Outlaws of the Pacific Northwest

Outlaws
of the
Pacific Northwest

Bill Gulick

CAXTON PRESS
Caldwell, Idaho
2000

Library of Congress Cataloging-in-Publication Data

Bill Gulick, 1916 —
    Outlaws of the Pacific Northwest: / Bill Gulick.--1st ed.
        p. cm.
    Includes bibliographical references and index.
    ISBN 0-87004-396-x (paper)
    1. Outlaws--Northwest, Pacific--Biography--Anecdotes. 2. Frontier and pioneer
life--Northwest, Pacific--Anecdotes. 3. Northwest, Pacific--History--19th century--
Anecdotes. 4. Northwest, Pacific--Biography--Anecdotes. I. Title.
I. Title.
F852.G85 2000
979.5'041'0922--dc21   99-057972

Lithographed and bound in the United States of America
CAXTON PRESS
Caldwell, Idaho
165702

In 1950, a new Western novel appeared on bookstore shelves around the nation. *Bend in the Snake*, the first book by a young writer named Bill Gulick, was so well received that it was made into a major motion picture—*Bend in the River*, starring Jimmy Stewart.

During the past half century, Bill Gulick has written more than thirty fiction and nonfiction Western books, several screenplays and dozens of newspaper and magazine articles. He is one of the legendary figures in Western writing.

To commemorate the 50th anniversary of his first book, we dedicate *Outlaws of the Pacific Northwest* to Bill Gulick, and his charming wife, Jeannie.

The Publishers

CONTENTS

Illustrations x

Introduction xi

Chapter 1 – Chief Bigfoot—Fact or Fancy? 1

Chapter 2 –Dave Updyke, Idaho's Bogus Basin Sheriff 13

Chapter 3 – Ferd Patterson—Dandy Gunman of Idaho City 29

Chapter 4 – Richard Bogle: Refuge for His Race 47

Chapter 5 – Josephine Wolf: Walla Walla's Genteel Madam 55

Chapter 6 – Henry Plummer—Outlaw Sheriff of Alder Gulch . . . 67

Chapter 7 – Days of Power For the Plummer Gang 83

Chapter 8 – The Infernal Triangle 97

Chapter 9 – Judgment Day for the Plummer Gang 109

Chapter 10 – Aftermath—Cleaning Up the Human Debris 127

Chapter 11 – Murder in Hells Canyon: The Chinese Massacre . 135

Chapter 12 – Hank Vaughan—The Amiable Horsethief 147

Chapter 13 – Harry Orchard: Miners' Union Hit Man 161

Chapter 14 – The Bill Haywood Trial. 181

Bibliography 193

Index 195

The Author 199

ILLUSTRATIONS

Northwest Map xiv
Silver City, Idaho Territory, 1866 3
Bigfoot allegedly was killed in a rocky canyon in the Owyhee
    Mountains, on the road from Boise City to Silver City 7
Billy McConnell 15
Camp Lyon guarded trail from Idaho mines to California 21
Walter's Ferry as it may have looked in the 1860s 23
Ferd Patterson 31
Sumner Pinkham 33
Territorial Prison, Idaho City, 1860s.. 43
St. Louis Hotel, Walla Walla, Washington 57
Josephine Wolfe Monument, Walla Walla Cemetery 63
Nathaniel P. Langford 99
Hill Beachy 111
Plummer was hanged on the gallows he built while sheriff 123
Store where Plummer Gang members were hanged 133
Chinese miners often worked claims abandoned by whites 137
Chinese encampment at Delamar, Idaho 143
Chinese miners work a claim in the Boise Basin 145
Frank Steunenberg 163
The Steunenberg home shortly after the blast 164
Harry Orchard 165
Western Federation of Miners Union officials were arrested
    in Colorado and spirited to Idaho in a special train ... 183

INTRODUCTION

Why the outlaws of the Pacific Northwest are so little known long has puzzled me. My research indicates that during gold-boom and settlement days, Montana, Idaho, Oregon, and Washington certainly had their share of violent characters who are as well qualified for an "Outlaw Hall of Ill Fame" as candidates promoted by other communities.

The regional folklorist, Russell Blankenship, best stated the problem in his book *And There Were Men*, (Alfred A. Knopf, 1942), when he wrote:

> "The Northwest had its quota of desperadoes . . . but the glory of our outlaws has been dimmed by colorless chroniclers."

Which is to say that if Ned Buntline, Bret Harte, Mark Twain, Zane Grey, Max Brand, and the scores of lurid writers who immortalized Billy the Kid, Wild Bill Hickok, and Gunfight at the O.K. Corral in other parts of the country had applied their talents to the violent characters and events of the Pacific Northwest, our region would have taken its proper place in history.

Though I never met Russell Blankenship, I did know his daughter, Nancy Pryor, who became a research specialist in the Washington State Library in Olympia. Following her retirement, Nancy returned to her roots in Walla Walla, where she gave generously of her skills to Penrose Library at Whitman College until her death a few years ago. We often talked about her father, who had been a Professor of English at the University of Washington, and his theory that it had been dull writers (not dull outlaws) who denied the Pacific Northwest the aura of ill fame it deserves.

Some day, we agreed, somebody ought to write a book about our badmen . . .

The "some day" seems to be now. The "somebody" designated to redeem the failings of the "colorless chroniclers" seems to be me . . .

The very word "Outlaw" implies the existence of a Code of Laws to be violated and officials appointed, elected, or named to enforce it. Also implied is the existence of courts, judges, and legal systems in which justice may be obtained.

In the Pacific Northwest during the first half of the last century, none of those entities existed. During the second half, the small population and vast distances of the area made law enforcement by territorial and state governments weak and ineffectual. The absence of a formalized Code of Laws and a government to enforce it did not mean that people living in the area would tolerate anarchy. For if there is a single trait that distinguishes residents of the United States from those of other countries, it is that they believe in self-government and will not put up very long with a community whose residents are not law-abiding.

During Oregon Trail days from the 1830s onward, every westering wagon train elected a council and a captain who made and enforced strict rules of behavior. Following the discovery of gold in the 1850s, every camp set up standards for filing claims, allocating water to placer mines, and respecting property rights. At first, the travelers and the prospectors were too busy to waste time enforcing these rules, assuming their fellow citizens would honor and obey them. When they did not, the violators were haled before a peoples' court, which quickly tried and punished the transgressors with either banishment, public whipping, or hanging.

Call it "Vigilante" justice, if you will. At the time, it was the only kind of justice available. When Mark Twain, who spent several years in Nevada during its gold-boom period, was asked if innocent men might not have been hanged now and then by vigilantes, he replied sardonically:

"Those days, there weren't many innocent men in Nevada."

In addition to the usual motive of greed, two factors not

so prevalent in other parts of the country contributed to the lawlessness of the Pacific Northwest: politics and the Civil War.

Under the Joint Occupancy Treaty in effect between 1818 and 1846, the citizens of both the United States and Great Britain were allowed to roam at will across a vast region. It extended from the northern border of Spanish California on the 38th Parallel, to the southern border of Russian Alaska at the 54th and from the Pacific Ocean on the west to the summit of the Rocky Mountains to the east. Over all this huge expanse of land, no organized form of government existed.

Gold was discovered in California in 1848. Miners rushed to what would become Oregon, Washington, Idaho, and Montana in the early 1860s. Territories were organized, with governors appointed by the president of the United States, who by then was deeply involved in the Civil War. Hoping to avoid involvement in the conflict, many Northern, Southern, and border state residents emigrated west—roughly an equal mix of Republicans and Democrats, Union and Confederate sympathizers. Understandably, they took their politics and beliefs with them, which would cause just as much strife and bloodshed in this new land as they had caused at home.

For example, one Idaho politician accused of saying, "All Democrats are horse thieves!" Vehemently denied having made the statement. "What I said, and am prepared to prove," he declaimed, "was that all horse thieves are Democrats!"

In recent years, revisionist historians have found it politically correct to tell us how badly our ancestors behaved and how much better they would have managed past events, if they had been there at that place and time. Maybe so. But in the dozen or so accounts that follow, I have tried to present these outlaw stories as they were recorded by the "colorless chroniclers" of the day, hoping that by a bit of judicious editing, condensing, and filtering through my own biased vision of the past, I may add a bit of color to the tales.

BILL GULICK

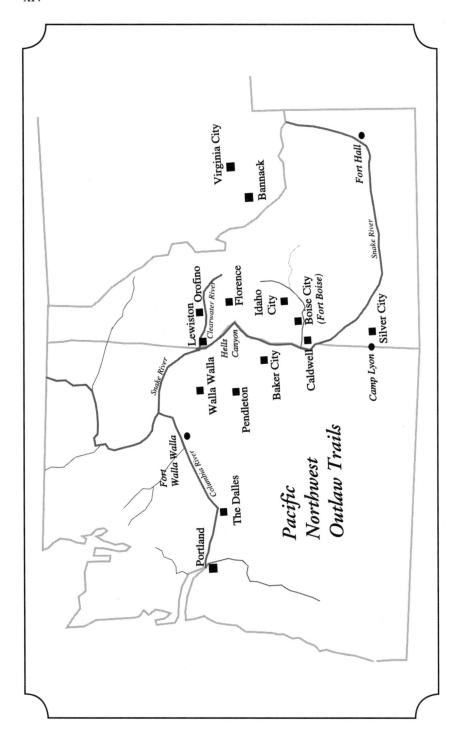

1

CHIEF BIGFOOT—FACT OR FANCY?

O nce the green patches of irrigated land south of Snake River are left behind, today's traveler discovers neither the country nor the rocky, rutted road climbing toward the 6,200-foot town of Silver City have changed much since the first stagecoach passed this way en route from Boise City to Chico, California, in 1865. The sagebrush, the bunchgrass, the canyons filled with tumbled red rocks, the timbered Owyhee Mountains rising ahead, and the brooding emptiness of vast reaches of space make one feel that if ever there were a region ideally suited to an Indian ambush, this is it.

The feeling is solidly based on fact. The area that today includes much of southwestern Idaho and eastern Oregon was the domain of the fabled Chief Bigfoot. Though historians seriously doubt that such a monster ever existed, the havoc wrought by the band of savages Bigfoot supposedly led in their long, bitter war against the whites was brutally real.

In the early 1860s, rich deposits of silver were found in the region. As the Owyhee mines boomed and travel increased along the inland route to California, stage stations, trading settlements, and ranches sprang up every ten miles or so along the long, lonely desert road through southwestern Idaho, eastern Oregon, and northern Nevada. These became prime raiding targets for roving bands of Paiute, Bannock, and Shoshone Indians, who had not yet been "settled" on reservations.

The military post of Fort Boise was established adjacent to the townsite of that city, in August 1863, for the express purpose of protecting travelers, miners, and settlers living in the area. But the Civil War raging in the East drained the fort of troops and funds, so its undermanned garrison could do little to prevent or punish raids by hostiles along the road south.

Poor communications and vast distances compounded the problem. News of an attack on a Reynolds Creek ranch, a stage station in the Jordan Valley, or 100 unarmed Chinamen traveling afoot across the eastern Oregon desert, required two to four days to reach the military post. Once the decision was made to send out a punitive force, more days were needed to organize and ride; still more to reach the area in which the attack had occurred. By then, the hostiles had vanished like last week's dust.

As one newspaper editor sarcastically commented, the Army's mode of going after raiding Indians was "Like hunting ducks with a brass band."

Loudly proclaiming they could do the job better, intrepid groups of citizens now and again organized their own bands of volunteers, collecting money, ammunition, food, and horses from public-spirited townspeople, electing leaders, making elaborate campaign plans, and then sallying forth to settle the Indian problem once and for all. Since few working merchants, miners, or ranchers could spare the time to go hostile-hunting, these "volunteers" often were loafers, saloon hangers-on, or rowdies looking for excitement. They were the breed of men that loudly recommended killing all Indians, regardless of sex or age, because "nits make lice." Some even proposed putting a cash bounty on every Indian scalp taken, though there is no evidence that any such bounty was ever approved or paid in that part of the country. But when the action began, their bloodthirstiness usually abated in direct proportion to the number of arrows and bullets fired in their direction.

On one occasion, a Boise City group of hostile-hunters calling themselves the "Ada County Volunteers" collected $3,000

Idaho State Historical Society 77-19.15
Silver City, Idaho Territory, 1866.

in cash and supplies. They spent three weeks in the field, sent glowing dispatches detailing their glorious doings to Boise City for publication in the paper, and then returned to bask in accumulated glory. But the truth soon leaked out. Not a single hostile had been sighted nor a single shot fired in anger. Once south of the Snake, the volunteers had stopped to "drill and discipline," laid out a racetrack, set up targets, uncorked bottles, and had themselves a high old time. Understandably, the Boise City merchants underwrote no more Indian hunts.

On another occasion, the "Owyhee Volunteers" actually did stir up some Indians who were in a fighting mood. Suffering a stinging defeat, the whites found themselves surrounded in a basin deep in the mountains and very likely would have been "massacred" had not their loyal Indian scout, Bruneau Jim, managed to slip through the lines of the attackers under cover of darkness and make his way on foot fifty miles to the mining camp of Flint, where a relief force was raised to lift the siege.

Ironically, when the church bells of Flint started ringing to signal that help was needed, many of the miner residents were in hardrock tunnels far underground, fighting each other with pistols, rifles, and live steam because one company allegedly had trespassed into a silver vein claimed by another company. When told about the Indian attack, the combatants on both sides suspended hostilities, formed a rescue party, and lifted the siege. By the time they returned to town, the squabble over the invaded vein had been settled peacefully in court by a bloodless judicial ruling.

Two years later, sad to relate, Bruneau Jim was murdered by four white men when he objected to their ravishment of two Indian women who were with him. Among volunteers and newsmen who remembered Bruneau Jim's heroism, sentiment strongly favored hanging the four white men. But sentiment did not prevail. Three of the four men were held as material witnesses, while the fourth, John Brady, was tried on the reduced charge of manslaughter. After two juries failed to convict him, he was set free.

Chief Bigfoot, the alleged leader of all the hostile Indians in the area, was known by several names. Some years after his alleged demise, he was honored by having the town of Nampa, Idaho, named after him. "Nam-puh," in the Bannock tongue, supposedly means "Big-foot." He was also called "Oulux" and "We-ah-we-ha," which mean the same thing in other regional Indian dialects. In the tradition of all folklore giants, he was never seen; but whenever a horse or cow was stolen, a stage station or cabin raided, or an atrocity committed, his tracks were found in the vicinity.

Of the dozen or so contemporary references to Chief Bigfoot, the following account by T. J. Sutton, who accompanied an expedition led by Jeff Standifer against the Bannocks in 1863, is typical:

"Had cooler heads commanded, we should almost certainly have secured all the horses and probably the thieves as well, including, as I believe, the noted 'Bigfoot' who was their leader and boss horse thief of the plains.

"On looking over the grounds after the skirmish, we discovered the tracks of a band of Indians numbering ten or twelve who had crossed the river at that point two or three days before. We also discovered and measured Bigfoot's track, which was seventeen and a half inches long by six inches wide at the junction of the metatarsus with the toe. At that time we had no knowledge of the man, but the enormous size of his track attracted our attention and so roused our curiosity that careful measurements of its dimensions were made, and no little discussion indulged in as to whether it was a human track.

"A year or two later, the possessor of the abnormally sized foot had become famous because of his connection with and known leadership of gangs of Bannock horse thieves who raided the ranches of settlers whenever opportunity afforded. This continued down to 1868, when Bigfoot was allegedly killed in an encounter with a highwayman named Wheeler . . ."

Inspired by this account or their own lively imaginations, little boys in the area made something of a game of fashioning moccasins seventeen and a half inches long by six inches wide with which they could make Bigfoot tracks after committing pranks such as overturning outhouses, tying strings of cans to milk cow tails, or chasing late-night drunks home with whoops and hollers and threats to scalp them. The practice continues down to the present day. Now and again near wilderness areas hikers, hunters, and individuals not known for their probity come into the office of a small-town newspaper and excitedly tell its editor about their recent Bigfoot encounter, which they attempt to prove by strands of hair they have recovered from tree trunks or plaster casts of footprints made by a monster they just missed seeing.

Back in the 1860s, Chief Bigfoot was described by Idaho pioneer John Hailey in his book *History of Idaho* as being "six foot eight inches tall and weighing two hundred and eighty pounds." At that time, this would have been a very big man. Nowadays, of course, the description fits the average defensive linemen in the National Football League. So today's reports of Bigfoot sightings increase his height to eight feet and his weight to 600 pounds, though the length of his footprint remains the same.

Before relating the legendary duel in which Chief Bigfoot met his match, we must tell a smaller story, which we know is true. As a result of the raid led by Jeff Standifer, John Hailey wrote: "All the Indians were killed with the exception of one squaw and two boys, aged approximately six and twelve years old. The smaller boy was adopted by John Kelly, the violinist . . ."

Affectionately called "Fiddler John" by his thousands of mining-town friends in the West, John Kelly was Irish, a bachelor, and one of the most highly paid entertainers in the business. His lively jigs could set clumsy boots to clumping just as quickly as sentimental ballads like *My Mother's Grave* could bring lumps into choked-up throats. He was also a prudent man.

"The contract under which he played, Hailey writes, "included the installation of a swinging stage, or platform, swung by iron rods from the upper joists, several feet above the heads of those who might stand on the floor below. This platform was reached by a movable ladder, which, after he ascended, he pulled up out of reach of those below . . ."

High upon his aerie, Fiddler John was safe from stampedes, panics, and fights—which occurred almost nightly—and above the likely course of bottles and bullets that might damage his person or his precious violin. It was his habit, when bullets began to fly, to turn and face the disturbance, holding his violin behind him, so that the stray slug that shattered it first must pass through his own corpulent body.

Emotionally, he favored the cause of the South. After adopting the Indian boy, whom he named Willie, he had a tailor make the lad a little gray suit, representing a Confederate uniform. Willie had a well-knit frame and jet black eyes which fairly sparkled. His looks proclaimed him what he was, a full-blooded aborigine.

Kelly became father and mother to the little waif. He kept the youngster in his presence continually, and began at once a course of training to prepare the boy for the future that he had conceived for him. In a few months, the youth had

Wayne Cornell

Bigfoot allegedly met his match in the foothills of the Owyhee Mountains on the stage road between Boise City and Silver City.

developed into a contortionist of no mean ability, and nightly occupied a place with his adopted father, giving occasional exhibitions to vary the performance, thus adding interest to the attraction.

The boy eventually, either from inherent talent, his association with Kelly, or both, developed wonderful skill as a violinist. When eighteen, he equalled his instructor. But while on a visit to Ireland with his inseparable companion, he was taken with a congestive chill and died. Kelly had no children of his own, and while he related the story of the boy's life and death, his furrowed face was deluged with tears.

Chief Bigfoot's alleged demise marked the end of hostile depredations in southwestern Idaho, a region so remote and sparsely populated that it sometimes is called the "Forgotten Corner" of the region. An apocryphal "eyewitness" account entitled "Bigfoot's Last Fight," by William T. Anderson, was published serially in the *Idaho Statesman* in November 1878, ten years after the event. Since its style is more Wild West genre than factual history, it is repeated here only as a piece of folklore that incorporates many tall tales of the day, lightly salted with facts. Yet for a time it was so widely accepted as the truth that a group of pioneer descendants cast and erected a plaque on the banks of Snake River near the canyon in which Bigfoot supposedly was killed, relating the details of the duel.

John Wheeler, the highwayman, did live for a time in Silver City and was reputed to be a gunman. He once held up a stagecoach in eastern Oregon; and some years later was killed while attempting the same feat down in Arizona Territory. Salting these two facts as seasoning into his so-called "eyewitness" account written ten years after the event, William T. Anderson did what many other writers have done before and since: told a lurid tale that caught the interest of many readers and brought him a few weeks of journalistic fame.

The way Anderson tells the story, after lying in wait for three days, Wheeler trapped Bigfoot, challenged him, and the battle was on. The duel took place in what became known as Bigfoot Canyon, a few miles south of Snake River, on the stage route to Silver City. When the shooting ended and the gunsmoke cleared, Bigfoot lay prostrate in the dust, twelve bullets from a Henry rifle in his body. Though both his legs and one of his arms were broken, he still was considered so dangerous that when he asked for a drink of water, Wheeler replied:

"Hold on till I break the other arm, old rooster; then I'll give you a drink."

"Well, do it quick," Bigfoot said, "and give me a drink and let me die."

According to the account, Wheeler drew his pistol and broke Bigfoot's other arm, then went down to the creek, filled a canteen with water, and "placed it in the mouth of the Indian, who drank it all . . ."

Bigfoot then said he would like some whiskey. Wheeler replied that he had a small bottle of whiskey and ammonia, which he always carried in case of snakebite. Bigfoot said: "Give it to me quick; I'm getting blind." Wheeler handed him the pint flask.

"The Indian drank it, every drop, and then fell back apparently dead. After a few minutes he revived, and said that he was better . . ."

That a man with that many bullet holes in him could even hold that much fluid, let alone make the lengthy confession of his lurid life that he now made, shall not be questioned here. This was his story:

He had been born in the Cherokee Nation. His father, a white man named Archer Wilkinson, had been hanged for murder, but his mother, who was part Cherokee and part Negro, had been a good, religious woman. His name was Starr Wilkinson, but he had been called "Bigfoot" as long as he could remember. His height was six foot eight and one-half inches, he weighed more than 300 pounds, and his chest measured fifty-nine inches.

He had come west with an emigrant train in 1856, driving a wagon for his room and board. He fell in love with a young lady of the company, who thought a good deal of him until a smart, good-looking artist from New York joined the train. From the way the young lady turned cold toward him, Starr Wilkinson suspected that the artist had told her something bad about him. While camped near the Goose Creek Mountains, he and the artist went out to round up the stock one morning, they argued, and the artist admitted having made derogatory references to Wilkinson's parentage.

"This made me mad, and I told him if he called me that again I would kill him. So he drew his gun on me and repeated it. I was unarmed, but started at him. He shot me in the side but did not hurt me much, so I grabbed him and threw him down, and choked him to death, then threw him into Snake River, took his gun, pistol and knife, and ran off into the hills . . ."

Thus began Bigfoot's long, bloody career as a renegade leader of the hostiles. For a time, he said, Joe Lewis, instigator of the Whitman Massacre, had been his chief aide. Together, they had planned and carried out as deeds of vengeance the Ward Party Massacre (never mind that it took place two years before Starr Wilkinson started west), the Otter (Utter) Massacre, the eventual murder of the young lady who had jilted him, and countless other killings.

But now he had reached the end of the trail. Learning that Wheeler had a smattering of Cherokee blood in his veins, Bigfoot broke down and wept. Then he asked Wheeler to grant him two last requests.

The first was that no one be told of his death.

The second was that his body be buried where it could never be found.

John Wheeler agreed.

And Bigfoot died content.

Whether the eyewitness, William T. Anderson, also was in on the pact is not clear. But the fact that he waited ten years to write his story indicates that he was. If so, his dishonorable act in relating a story he had promised not to tell cannot be condoned simply by saying that writers, as a class, are a notoriously untrustworthy lot.

But this can be said for the highwayman, John Wheeler: He never told, and he buried Bigfoot's body so skillfully that its bones have never been found.

Credit for bringing what the white man called peace to this part of the country actually must be given to General George S. Crook, who here perfected the skills he later would use against the Apaches in the Southwest. Put in charge of the military district, he arrived in Boise City on December 11, 1866, replacing Colonel L. H. Marshall, who, to put it mildly, was making no headway against the hostiles. In General Crook's own words:

> "Indian affairs could not have been worse. The whole country was in a state of siege . . ."

One week after his arrival, a band of Indians made a raid

near the mouth of the Boise River, twenty miles west of the fort. Crook wrote:

"So I took Capt. Perry's company of the 1st Cavalry and left with one change of underclothes, toothbrush, etc., and went to investigate matters, intending to be gone a week. But I got interested after the Indians and did not return there again for over two years . . . "

Persistence was Crook's chief virtue and the secret to his success. A man who did not drink, smoke, use coffee or tea, he disliked fancy uniforms, spirited horses, and red tape. His usual mount was a mule, his dress that of an outdoorsman. His passion was hunting wild game; his job hunting wild Indians. And for him the hunt did not end until the quarry was in the bag.

Winter and summer, spring and fall, in all extremes of temperature, weather, and terrain across southwestern Idaho, eastern and central Oregon, northern Nevada, and northern California, he stayed "interested after Indians . . ." for two years. Remaining in the field while supplies were sent out to his forces, he wore the Indians down until the scattered, starving, decimated bands one-by-one gave up their hopeless resistance. By the time the last pathetic group surrendered in July 1868, an estimated two-thirds of their people had died. But General Crook had done the job he was being paid to do.

Though not a believer in folklore giants, Crook did record in memoirs written many years later the sighting of an Indian called "Bigfoot" somewhere in the desert of eastern Oregon, southwestern Idaho, or northern Nevada. Identified as a Paiute, the Indian stood over six feet tall, Crook wrote, and was so fleet afoot he could run down jackrabbits. Because his moccasin track was fourteen and a half inches long, he was called "Bigfoot" by his people, but in no other way did he resemble the legendary monster . . .

Under any name (Sasquatch, Yeti, the Abominable Snowman, or variations thereof) the Bigfoot legend has refused to die.

Its basic tenet is that somewhere in the remote reaches of mountain wilderness areas all over the world, a huge, hairy, powerful creature exists that no man ever has seen and lived to identify. Even more remarkable is the fact that no skeletal or fossil remains of such a creature have ever been found.

When it is pointed out to believers in the Bigfoot legend that scientists have found and identified dinosaur skeletons millions of years old, even though these prehistoric monsters became extinct aeons ago, the believers reply vaguely by saying that the Bigfoot species is very secretive about where it buries its dead. Then they ask the unanswerable question:

"Can you prove Bigfoot doesn't exist?"

No one can, of course. During the thirty-five years that I have kept a Bigfoot file, I have found no credible piece of proof that such a creature does exist. Still, I retain an open mind, for I count as good friends several regional newspaper writers and a venerable "mountain man" whose probity I cannot challenge who do believe in the existence of the creature. Nothing would please me more than to receive a cellular phone call from one of them camped in a wilderness camp, saying, "I've just met a friendly Bigfoot, who has agreed to be interviewed. Shall I put him on the line?"

My first question would be: "Why did you decide to join the human race?"

2

DAVE UPDYKE, IDAHO'S
BOGUS BASIN SHERIFF

Nestled in the mountains twenty miles northeast of Boise, Idaho, is a beautiful high valley called the Bogus Basin Ski Area. The name does not refer to local false claims about the quality of its snow, which is excellent, but to a cottage industry and a sheriff during its gold-boom days, both as bogus as they could be.

Isolated as mining communities were during the 1860s, obtaining a medium of exchange for transacting everyday business was a problem. The nearest mint at which gold or silver could be turned into coins was in San Francisco, with at least six months required before precious metal dug in Idaho could be shipped there and returned as hard cash. Qualified assayers who could tell the merchant whether the ounce of gold dust he had accepted in payment for a transaction was worth $16, $14, $12, $10, $8, or—as one editor sarcastically put it "of no value until you start plastering the walls of your house"—were few and far between. So for some unscrupulous men—of which there were more than a few around—turning dross into gold became a major, profitable occupation.

Designated a territory in 1863, the capital of Idaho first was located in the northern town of Lewiston, then was hijacked 300 miles south to Boise City. Governor Caleb Lyon of Lyonsdale, New York, (as he insisted on signing his name) went duck hunting on the nearby Snake River one afternoon while the records were being stolen by southern Idaho legislators. Following this bit of chicanery, Caleb Lyon got aboard a stagecoach supposedly headed for Boise City by way of Walla Walla. But instead Lyon went to Portland, San Francisco, Washington City, and then Lyonsdale, New York. Fatigued from his travels, he rested there for six months, went back to Washington City and picked up $30,000 in cash with which to "treat with the Indians," then returned to Idaho Territory.

Lyon stayed in Idaho just long enough to accept a silver brick cast in his honor by the mine owners in the Owyhee district, and a gold brick fabricated by corporate interests in the Rocky Bar area. He then felt it necessary to return to the East, where he attempted to explain to the government how he happened to lose the $30,000 in Indian funds he was supposed to disburse. Though his story that the money had been stolen from a belt under his coat while he was sleeping on a train sounded a bit lame to the authorities, no charges were brought against Lyon.

If an account of these antics inclines today's reader to think that government in Idaho was in a state of confusion during the 1860s, citizens living in that place and time would have called the term too mild. "Chaos" or "anarchy" would have been more appropriate words. In any event, it was clear that if a semblance of law and order were to be brought to the region, such a desired state was not going to be achieved by appointed or elected officials.

Thus, the rise of the Payette Valley Vigilantes.

Called the "Vegetable Peddler," twenty-one-year-old Billy McConnell earned the nickname on his first visit to the gold-boom community of Placerville when he parked a wagon loaded with fresh produce adjacent to the town square. He sold dollar-a-dozen roasting ears, two-dollar cantaloupes, and five-dollar watermelons so fast to the fresh-produce-hungry miners that he decided more money could be made raising food in Idaho's valleys than grubbing for gold in Idaho's hills. Becoming part of a community of honest, hard-working farmers and stockmen settling in the fertile Payette Valley, thirty miles northwest of Boise City, William J. McConnell (as he was formally named) soon became its recognized leader, despite his youth.

Infesting the gold camps and spilling over into the adjoining towns and rural areas at that time was a class of men called "roughs."

The distinguishing characteristic of "roughs" was that they would rather steal than work. Defrauding merchants by coating lead shavings with a thin layer of gold dust, then passing the bogus material off as the real thing, was considered by the commercial world

Idaho State Historical Society 74-190.1
Billy McConnell
"The Vegetable Peddler"

to be just as serious a crime as stealing a horse was in the ranching world. As honest citizens, Billy McConnell and his neighbors assumed that the law and its representatives would protect them. But they soon learned otherwise.

Triggering Billy McConnell's first lesson with the roughs was the loss of a bay horse from a pack-string during a trip to Placerville in July 1864. Three months later, he saw the horse in a Boise City livery stable owned by a man named Dave Updyke. Telling the livery stable owner that the horse was his, McConnell asked him where he got it. Oh, he'd bought it from some drifter whose name he did not remember, Updyke said, but since he had paid for it and now possessed it, he was not going to give it up unless forced to do so.

Tracing the animal back through several previous owners— none of whom had bothered to get a bill of sale—Billy McConnell finally identified the man he felt had first stolen it as a rough named Gil Peters—who just happened to work for Dave Updyke.

"There was no way I could prove he was the thief," Billy told a friend, "But I'm dead certain he was."

Forced to hire a lawyer, go into court, and bring witnesses who would testify that the bay horse indeed was his, Billy McConnell spent two days unraveling the legal red tape necessary to get the horse back. The horse was worth fifty dollars. Legal costs came to seventy dollars.

As he led the horse along the street after recovering it, a crowd of roughs loafing in front of a saloon—including Gil Peters—jeered at him and made insulting remarks as he passed. So he stopped and made a brief speech.

"I can catch any thief that ever walked these prairies," he said. "The next man who steals a horse from me is my Injun. There will be no lawsuit about it."

Then, amid much jeering and laughter, he moved on . . .

A few nights later, four good mules and five horses—worth at least $2,000—disappeared from Billy McConnell's farm and the farms of two of his neighbors. The sign indicated that the theft had been accomplished by four men. The animals had been driven west along what was known as the Brownlee Ferry Trail. In all likelihood, the thieves planned to drive the horses and mules across the Blue Mountains to the Columbia River Valley, where they could be sold without any need to prove ownership. Meeting with his neighbors, McConnell spoke bluntly.

"It comes down to this, gentlemen. Either we teach these devils a lesson or we give up and move out. It's as simple as that."

To a man, his neighbors agreed.

McConnell and two friends rode west, next morning, and were gone two weeks. When they returned, the four stolen mules and the five horses were in their care and were turned over to their rightful owners. One of the men had a bandaged arm; he had taken a fall upon sharp rocks, he said. No questions were asked or answered . . .

Meanwhile, Dave Updyke, the livery stable owner, had

gotten himself elected sheriff of Ada County. Using the livery stable as a front, Updyke assembled a band of men who the public had good reason to believe were responsible for most of the robberies and murders committed in the surrounding area. Though the Updyke Gang did its best to cover its tracks so that no positive evidence could be found against them, some of the crimes attributed to them were not noted for their brilliance. For example, historian Nathaniel Langford writes:

"Early in the fall of 1864, a gentleman by the name of Parks went to Idaho, and in Owyhee county purchased and located claims on several quartz lodes, specimens of which he selected to exhibit to his Eastern friends, and packed carefully in a valise. Coming to Boise City, preparatory to his departure for the States, he passed through the streets with the heavy valise in his hands, which, being observed by the 'Opdyke gang,' was supposed by them to contain a large quantity of gold dust. He remained in Boise four or five days, and was narrowly watched by the roughs."

In mining circles then as now, quartz samples assaying $800 to the ton of "country rock," would be considered rich ore, well worth working. But the contents of a valise containing fifty pounds of such samples, if crushed and refined, would yield only twenty dollars worth of gold—not much of a haul for a hard-working gang. Nevertheless, the Updyke crowd stalked Parks, followed the stagecoach caught by him, and seven miles east of town, caused the driver to stop, fired upon Parks, rifled his pockets of two or three hundred dollars in money, and departed with the much coveted valise. Their chagrin at finding it to contain mere quartz specimens, may be better imagined than described.

A week after the badly wounded Parks was brought back to Boise City, he died. Being a Mason, he was buried with full ceremonial honors by his friends, who soon found evidence that a rough named Charley Marcus and three other members of the Updyke Gang had been involved in the attack. But since evidence was not proof and Sheriff Updyke refused to act, no arrests were made.

The next outrage in which Upyke was involved was the murder and robbery, in Port-Neuf Canyon, of five coach passengers from Montana in the summer of 1865. It was known that Updyke confederates furnished arms and ammunition for the party and shared in the booty.

Again, since there was no proof acceptable to Sheriff Updyke, he refused to investigate a stage robbery in which five people had been killed and $75,000 worth of gold had been stolen. Instead, he decided to go after the Payette Valley Vigilantes, who were engaging in such deplorably illegal activities as running down horse thieves and bogus dust operators.

Backed by a court order for the arrest of Billy McConnell and other suspected vigilante leaders, Constable Short, an Updyke assistant, rallied a crowd of well-armed deputies from among his Democratic friends in Boise City and rode toward Horseshoe Bend on the Payette River, taking the long way round because of the deep snowdrifts covering the intervening hills. Learning of the expedition, one of McConnell's friends in Boise breasted the drifts, crossed the ridges by the shorter route, and warned McConnell and his friends that a *posse comitatus* was coming to get them.

"Well," McConnell said quietly, "if it's trouble they want, we'll meet them halfway."

Rounding up his neighbors, McConnell soon raised a force of fifty men, took to the trail, surprised the posse as its members rested at a roadhouse, and challenged Constable Short to show his hand. In the bitter, confused, angry confrontation that followed, violence was averted by only the slimmest of margins.

"My God, Billy," Constable Short pleaded, "let's not have any shooting over this!"

"There won't be any shooting unless your crowd starts it," McConnell said grimly. "You've got a warrant for my arrest, I'm told."

"That's right."

"What made you think you'd need a mob of roughs backing you when you served it?"

"Well, talk was you'd make trouble—"

"So you rounded up a gang of drunken, gun-packing roughs that have been bragging all over Boise that they were going to rub out Billy McConnell and his farmer friends—"

"Now, Billy, these men are legally appointed deputies. I warn you against any attempt to resist arrest. I call on you all to give up your guns."

"Serve your warrants, Constable. My friends and I respect the law. We'll appear in the Boise City court at any hour and day we're requested to do so. We'll answer all charges brought against us. But we will not surrender our guns."

Eventually, both groups dispersed and went home. A few days later, McConnell and the alleged Vigilante leaders rode into Boise City, employed legal counsel, went to court and succeeded in getting the charges against them dismissed. Some months later, the final word to the fiasco was written when a bill introduced in the Territorial Legislature for the payment of expenses entailed in arresting and bringing the Payette Vigilance Committee to trial went down to a thumping defeat.

But by then, Dave Updyke was in deep trouble. . .

Displeased with the way their sheriff was handling both the physical and financial matters of the county, the commissioners brought charges against him, accusing him first of letting a prisoner escape, second of making off with $1,100 dollars in public funds. When indicted by a grand jury on both charges, Updyke paid the amount he was accused of stealing and resigned as sheriff, with the result that the charges were withdrawn.

Whether his next venture was an attempt to get back in the good graces of the community, a scheme to make money, or undertaken for lack of anything better to do, is not clear. But whatever its motive, it was publicized in the *Idaho Statesman* in Boise City, Idaho Territory, February 27, 1866:

"The fund raised by public description to arm, mount and supply a group of volunteers to go Indian-hunting now totals $3000. At a recent meeting, the name 'Ada Volunteers' was chosen; Dave C. Updyke, former sheriff, was elected Captain of the group, Chas. Ridgely Lieutenant. Within the week, some 25 well-armed, well-mounted men will head for the Snake country under Captain Updyke's leadership.

"Good hunting, boys!"

Captain Updyke's plan of campaign as he revealed it during fund-raising events held at Boise City saloons sounded like it would get excellent results. He intended to lead his troops south, he said, cross the Snake River, and bring the Indians to battle in the Reynolds Creek area, where they had been raising so much hell lately. With any luck at all, he predicted, he and his bully boys should be able to kill forty or fifty redskins. Then they would swing upriver and make a clean sweep of everything from Reynolds Creek to the Bruneau Valley, round up two or three hundred captives, and the area's Indian troubles would be over. All without federal help, mind you. Dig deep, gentlemen! It's for a worthy cause!

According to reports appearing in newspapers during the next three weeks, the Ada County Indian-Exterminating Expedition was getting along swimmingly. Updyke had led his well-armed, well-mounted, well-supplied fighting men south to Snake River, crossed it, then had wisely camped for a few days while he taught his troops discipline by extensive drilling, marksmanship by gruelling shooting sessions, and horsemanship by prolonged hours in the saddle.

Ready now for any enemy, he headed the column eastward with the firm intention of giving battle to the Bruneaus. However, messages hastily sent by Governor Lyon (who was trying to negotiate a peace treaty so that he could disburse some money), Major Marshall (who with 100 soldiers was guarding the governor), and by a man named Jennings (who was said to possess a petition signed by a large number of Owyhee district citizens begging the Volunteers *not* to shoot

Wayne Cornell

Camp Lyon was located in this meadow on the Idaho-Oregon border. The tiny military post was established to protect the road connecting southern Idaho mines with Nevada and California points.

their peace-abiding Bruneaus), persuaded Captain Updyke to turn his column in a southwesterly direction, where it seemed more likely *really* hostile Indians could be found.

The Ada Volunteers had ridden as far as the new Army post of Camp Lyon, it was reported, seeing no Indians, but had found Captain Walker and a contingent of Regular Army troops stationed there, who claimed they had things well in hand. Being refused a replenishment of ammunition and supplies by the penurious quartermaster, the brave but weary volunteers had no course left them but to turn about and come back to Boise City.

"The Ada Volunteers returned this week after being out twenty-four days without finding any Indians, reported the *Statesman*. At present, all the Indians appear to be gone from the area . . . this is no fault of the Volunteers . . ."

Indeed, it was not, Billy McConnell and his Payette Valley

neighbors agreed with many a chuckle, wondering aloud if Dave Updyke and his bully boys would take editor Jim Reynolds' sly comment straight or read a double meaning into it as they did.

As the days passed, indignant denials of Captain Updyke's war dispatches began to filter back to Boise City and tarnish the glory of the intrepid Volunteers. The expedition had never even *looked* for Indians, Reynolds Creek settlers claimed. There had been no messages from Major Marshall or Governor Lyon. There had been no petition signed by the Owyhee district citizens and delivered by Jennings. Nor had the war party ever moved off the sagebrush flat south of Snake River, upon which it had first camped, until it started the return trip to Boise City.

What actually had happened, that the men had made camp, cleared a race track grounds on the sage-covered flat, and then had spent the next two weeks racing horses, shooting at marks, eating, drinking, and having themselves such a high old time that no hostile Indian could have bought himself a fight unless he had offered to pay them by the hour for it in gold. And then, when ammunition, food, and whiskey were at last exhausted, they had come home.

Since this was the way most amateur Indian-hunting expeditions ended those days, the only after-effects of the fiasco ordinarily would have been a lack of enthusiasm on the part of the business community to contribute money to future efforts. But as Langford tells the story, the Updyke Gang got greedy:

> "A man by the name of Joseph Aden was employed to pack the stores, for which purpose eleven ponies were provided and placed in his charge, with the understanding that he should receive them in part payment for his services. In pursuance of that agreement, he immediately branded and ranched them."

Joining the Ada Volunteers was a nineteen-year-old youth man named Rueben Raymond, who had just been discharged

Wayne Cornell

Volunteers from Boise City camped on the flats south of the Snake River and held shooting contests and horse races, instead of hunting Indians in the distant Owyhee Mountains. This photograph of Walter's Ferry, on the Snake, has been modified to show how the area probably looked in the 1860s.

from the Army at Fort Boise. Liked by everybody, he was good-hearted, honest, and trustworthy, just the sort of idealistic young man to offer his services to such a noble cause as the Indian-hunting expedition appeared to be.

Too naive and innocent to see evil in any act or person, "Honest Rube," as he sometimes was called because of his habit of questioning an outlandish statement by asking incredulously, "Honest?", could always be depended upon to tell the truth. When Dave Updyke and a man named Drake tried to cheat Joseph Aden out of the eleven ponies he thought were his by practicing "constructive ownership," the quarrel wound up in court.

Asked to testify, Rube Raymond resisted the pressures being brought on him by the Updyke crowd, telling the simple truth as he perceived it. So far as he knew, he said, the ponies belonged to Joseph Aden.

The Updyke Gang got very angry with him. On the morning

of April 3, 1865, a few days after the examination, while Raymond was employed in a stall in Updyke's stable, John C. Clark, a noted rough, stepped before the stall with a revolver in his hand, and commenced cursing Raymond. Updyke and several of his associates, together with a number of good citizens, were standing near. Clark finally threatened Raymond.

"I am entirely unarmed," said Raymond, at same time pulling open his shirt bosom, "but if you wish to shoot me down like a dog, there is nothing to hinder you. Give me a chance, and I will fight you in any way you choose, though I have nothing against you."

Clark covered Raymond for a moment or more, with his pistol, and then cried, "I will shoot you, anyway." Taking deliberate aim, he fired and killed Raymond on the spot.

Feeling against John Clark for this unprovoked murder ran so high in the crowd of onlookers, that he was in danger of being lynched on the spot. Immediately charged with murder and placed under arrest, he was taken not to the county jail, from which his friends might help him escape, but to the military post of Fort Boise, where, with the commandant's permission, he was confined to the guardhouse.

For the next two days and nights, Boise City was a seething cauldron as law-and-order-loving citizens demanded that justice be done, while Updyke and his supporters made dire threats of the revenge they would take if John Clark were harmed. Until then, no active vigilante committee had existed in the Boise City. All the same, even the Updyke crowd felt that the accused man was much safer in the Fort Boise guardhouse than he would have been in the county jail.

Two mornings later, Clark's body was found suspended from an improvised gibbet of three poles not far from the fort. Pinned to one of the poles was a note which read:

No. 1.
Justice has now commenced her righteous work. This suffering community, which has already lain too long under the bane of ruffianism, shall now be renovated of its THIEVES and ASSASSINS. Forbearance has at last

ceased to be a virtue, and an outraged community has solemnly resolved on SELF PROTECTION.

Let this man's fate be a terrible warning to all his kind, for the argus eye of Justice is no more sure to see than her arm will be certain to strike.

The soil of this beautiful valley shall no longer be desecrated by the presence of THIEVES and ASSASSINS. This fatal example has no terror for the innocent, but let the guilty beware, and not delay too long, and take warning.

XXX

Tuesday morning, the *Statesman* published an account of the lynching. It read:

"Between the hours of one and two o'clock Saturday morning a party of men, numbering from fifteen to twenty-five, attacked the guard on the outside and entered the guard house at the same moment, then threw them down, smothered and pinioned them, threatening them with death if they resisted, while others entered the cell and took Clark away. After all were gone, one of the guards loosened himself and then his companions and gave the alarm at the garrison, but it was too dark to learn what direction had been taken by the captors. All the men were disguised so that they could not be recognized by the guard or by the remaining prisoners in the cell. No other disturbance whatever occurred, and nothing unusual was observed in town till daylight, when Clark was found hanging as before mentioned. Sheriff Duvall took charge of the body and buried it during the day.

"From all the circumstances attending the case, there can be no doubt but there is a most effective and determined organization of 'Vigilantes' in the community. The idea of taking the chances of overpowering the sentinels and guard at the post was a bold one, though at that time the men were all detailed on different expeditions, the officers all absent and not a sufficient number of men to do garrison duty. . . In regard to the crime of Clark, there is but one opinion in the community and that is he was guilty of cold blooded murder. Saturday morning there were some rather intemperate 'threats' indulged in by certain parties, particularly about burning down the town and the like, but nothing more has transpired . . ."

If the Boise City readers of the *Statesman* sensed a certain firmness and warning in Editor Jim Reynolds' account of the Clark lynching and its aftermath, they were most discreet in their public comments. It was common knowledge around Boise City that before riding off toward Rocky Bar, Dave Updyke and his friend Jake Dixon had sworn that they could name at least ten "stranglers" and that before the week was out they intended to return and "get even."

But Dave Updyke had started running too late. Exactly one week after the *Statesman* reported the Clark lynching, the Boise City paper relayed the following to its readers:

MORE OF THE VIGILANTES
UPDYKE AND DIXON HUNG

Mr. Dover and another gentleman arrived in town from Rocky Bar Sunday afternoon bringing the news that D. C. Updyke and Jake Dixon were hanging at Syrup Creek. Mr. Dover and his companion camped at Syrup Creek about dark on Saturday night, and had occasion to go down to the house, a short distance, and were surprised at finding no one living there, but Updyke suspended in the shed between the two houses. On the body was pinned the following card:

DAVE UPDYKE
The aider of Murderers and Horse Thieves.
XXX

The next morning they learned that Jake Dixon was also hanging to a tree a few miles down the creek. They could not tell how long the bodies had been there. Monday morning the

following card was found posted on Main Street, written in the
same handwriting as the one found on Clark a week ago:

DAVE UPDYKE

Accessory after the fact to the Port Neuf stage robbery.

Accessory and accomplice to the robbery of the stage
near Boise City in 1864.

Chief conspirator in burning property of the Overland
Stage line.

Guilty of aiding and assisting West Jenkins, the
murderer, and other criminals to escape, while you were
Sheriff of Ada County.

Accessory and accomplice in the murder of Raymond.

Threatening the lives and property of an already
outraged and suffering community.

Justice has overtaken you.

XXX

JAKE DIXON

Horse thief, counterfeiter and road agent generally.

A dupe and tool of Dave Updyke.

XXX

All the living accomplices in the above crimes are
known through Updyke's confession and will surely be
attended to.

The roll is being called.

XXX

Following the hasty exit of a number Boise City residents,
the roll call went unanswered.

3

FERD PATTERSON
DANDY GUNMAN OF IDAHO CITY

In his habit of dress, Ferdinand J. Patterson was something of a dandy. He normally wore a pair of custom-made, high-heeled boots that fitted his shapely feet to perfection, a pair of plaid trousers foxed with buckskin, a cashmere shirt, and a fancy silk vest, across the front of which dangled a heavy gold chain fashioned of California nuggets. Topping all this finery, except on extremely warm days, was a long frock coat made of heavy pilot-beaver cloth, tastefully trimmed with sea-otter fur.

His age was forty or so; his hands were the soft, white hands of the professional gambler; his hair was rusty red, his sharp, restless eyes were blue. Whatever the occasion, he always wore a gun.

Following the discovery of gold in northern Idaho in 1860, even bigger strikes were made in southern Idaho along the headwaters of the Boise River upstream from what eventually would become the capital of the newly-organized Territory of Idaho, Boise City. Boom-towns such as Placerville, Idaho City, Pioneerville, Atlanta, and Rocky Bar comprised what was called the "Boise Basin." Settled by a roughly equal mix of Democrats and Republicans, Northerners and Southerners, outlaws and law-abiding citizens—all of whom had brought their politics and prejudices with them. The Boise Basin was a lively place.

The fact that he went armed and was reputed to be quick-tempered may have been why no one ever accused Ferd Patterson of being a dandy—at least to his face. In height he stood an inch or two above six feet, weighed over 200 pounds, and carried himself like a man in top physical condition. These attributes may also have contributed to making him immune to criticism regarding his fondness for fine apparel.

With the Civil War ended in the summer of 1865, Ferd made no secret of the fact that he was a Southerner born and bred, that he mourned the South's lost cause. He said he would never stop grieving over the South's defeat or cease despising the people who brought it about. Exactly what section of the South he came from and why he had chosen to dwell in the Pacific Northwest were subjects he never discussed. Being the kind of man he was, it was he—not others—who generally channeled conversations.

Exciting things invariably happened wherever Ferd Patterson chanced to travel. Though it was said that he had engaged in a number of gunfights in California and western Oregon, not once had he been bested by another man. Even when haled into court to answer for his misdeeds, he had always emerged victorious.

When in good humor from drink, Ferd was not averse to giving vague, amiable confirmation to some of the fantastic tales being told about him:

"Well, yes, it is true," he admitted modestly, "that I, a lady companion, and a group of my friends took over an ocean steamer on the high seas between San Francisco and Portland. We did make its captain, its crew, and all the passengers dance to the tune we wanted to play. But it was all in fun, boys, good, clean fun.

"Hell, boys, sea voyages can be dull as dishwater unless the bar serves whiskey at all hours, the orchestra keeps playing, there's free food available whenever you want it, and no silly restrictions as to dancing, gambling, drinking and bed partners. All in fun, boys; all in fun. And fun was what we had.

"The gunfight in the Portland hotel with Captain Staples? Yes, there are a lot of conflicting stories about that and there's no use in my trying to straighten them out at this late date. Say he insulted me in a way no gentleman could permit. Say he waved the wrong flag at me. Say it was my honor and the South's honor at stake, plus a trivial personal item or two not worth mentioning. Guns were drawn, shots exchanged, he's dead, I'm not—and the court found the killing justified.

Idaho State Historical Society 111.A
Ferd Patterson

"The woman I was accused of scalping? Now that was a real laugh! I have an odd philosophy about women, boys, which I've developed over a long spell of years and a varied assortment of females. To state it briefly: when a woman's mine, she's mine—and she'd better not blink her eyelashes at anything else in pants. This one—never mind her name—did a bit of blinking. I warned her once, I warned her twice, and when that did no good, I decided to throw a scare into her.

"'Little lady,' I said, 'I've got Indian blood in me. When a squaw is unfaithful, I scalp her.' Well, I took out my knife, grabbed her by the hair, threw her down in a chair, and made a pass at her—just to scare her, mind. You know what the little fool did? Squirmed, that's what! And the first thing I knew, my knife whacked off a wee flake of skin.

"No, no, it isn't true that she came into court wearing a wig over her peeled head and testified in my behalf. Not true at all! But she did raise the bail money for me and begged me to forgive her for bringing charges. She writes me every week from Portland, wanting me to come back to her or let her come to Idaho, but I don't answer. After all the trouble she caused me, why should I do her a favor?

"Sumner Pinkham? Yes, I had a run-in with the Abolitionist son-of-a-bitch a couple of nights ago. He was drunk, celebrating a Union Party get-together with some of his Republican friends. No point in picking a fight with him then and there, I felt, though he did say a thing or two that got under my skin. Yes, it's true I warned him; I said:

"'Mr. Pinkham, I won't take that kind of talk off anybody—not even the ex-sheriff of Boise County. Next time we cross paths, keep a civil tongue in your head, sir, or I'll have to teach you a lesson in manners.'

"He's a tough customer, you say? Well, the breed isn't new to me. Not new at all . . ."

It was a damnable shame, Sumner Pinkham announced to all present in the saloon that evening. That with the Union saved, the martyred president newly laid in his grave, and Jefferson Davis, the traitorous leader of the Confederacy, in chains (he was captured while wearing his wife's clothes, by God, which just shows what kind of man *he* is!) —with all these great events having so recently transpired, it was a shame, a crime, a shabby show of patriotism that the loyal citizens of Idaho City had not made arrangements for a parade, a cannon, a brass band in full uniform, and a royal Fourth of July celebration next week, with fireworks, orations, and a huge mass picnic.

"But, Pink," a loyal citizen protested, "Idaho City ain't got no brass band! We got no instruments, no uniforms, no leader, no cannon—"

"Well, get 'em, I say!"

"Where?"

"Don't pester me with damn fool questions! I'll take care of the details myself. Just spread the word that at noon, come Fourth of July next week, Sumner Pinkham expects every loyal Union man, woman, and child in Boise County to fall in behind the brass band, which Mr. Pinkham will supply and lead himself, at the upper end of Main Street. We'll march through town in regular military formation, then go to a picnic spot where we'll have food and beer waiting."

"Hey, what about Warm Springs? That ain't too far out."

"Good! The very place! Let's see now—I'll take care of getting the band and the cannon, but we'll need committees on arrangements, speakers, beer, food . . ."

It had been Pinkham's notion that the commander at Fort Boise would be

Idaho State Historical Society 249-29
Sumner Pinkham

happy to send up the Army's brass band, a cannon, flags, and all the other paraphernalia necessary to a full dress parade. But because the patriotic citizens of Boise City already had arranged to stage a Fourth of July celebration of their own, all the commander sent was his regrets. Pinkham raged, pleaded, pulled strings—but to no avail.

"I can spare you a fifer," the colonel said, "a drummer and a flag—no more."

"Well, send 'em, then! But can't we have a cannon, too?"

"Sorry, Mr. Pinkham. It's against regulations to loan heavy ordnance to civilians."

Muttering dire threats that his political friends were going to hear about *this*, Sumner Pinkham grudgingly accepted the fifer, the drummer, and the flag, saying that what was lacking in military pomp and splendor would be made up for by civilian ingenuity and enthusiasm or, by God, he'd know the reason why.

As was usual on the single holiday of the year judged

important enough to suspend all mining work and close all business establishments except saloons, the drinking started early. After all, loyal Unionists had a great deal to celebrate. Because of a recent conflagration in Idaho City, the supply of fireworks was small, but in the constant bark of rifles, crack of pistols, boom of shotguns, and roar of blasting powder set off inside tin cans, this lack was scarcely noticed.

By noon, roughly half of Idaho City's population—plus sizable contingents of patriotic citizens come to town for the day from the outlying mining districts—had assembled at the upper end of Main Street on the outskirts of town. The other half, Democrats most of them, milled about on the boardwalks—between quick trips into convenient saloons for thirst-quenchers. They were prepared to boo, heckle, disrupt, confuse, and otherwise demonstrate that this was indeed a free country by turning what Union men bragged was to be the grandest parade ever into a complete fiasco.

Some minutes later than scheduled, Sumner Pinkham, who was to lead the march, conduct the band, and carry Old Glory, raised and dropped his right hand—which was the signal to fire the improvised cannon. This piece of ordnance—guaranteed by its inventors to make fully as big a boom as the biggest cannon in the Fort Boise arsenal—most certainly did make a satisfactory amount of noise.

Constructed of a length of rusty iron pipe, the cannon was aimed in the general direction of the town's business district and amply stuffed with blasting powder It had not been loaded with a projectile (though more than one man had suggested it would be great fun to drop a big ball of lead through the roof of a certain saloon notorious for the rabid Secessionists that patronized it, just to give the bastards a taste of what they had missed by not supporting Jeff Davis with deeds as well as words). Unfortunately, in seeking a maximum boom, the strength of the iron pipe had been overestimated. Thus, when the cannon went off, it went off in all directions. The editor of the local newspaper observed that:

> "It is a deplorable situation, when supposedly grown men of mature judgment get so carried away by patriotic

fervor (or was it whiskey, boys?) as to construct a noise-making instrument whose disintegration causes a rain of jagged metal to fly out in all directions at a high velocity. At least a dozen persons were wounded—fortunately none of them seriously—hundreds more were frightened out of their wits, a great number of windows were shattered, and a valuable milk cow belonging to Jake Hennessey (which was grazing a good three hundred yards away from the blast site) was killed outright, as a result of the explosion of the Union Party Fourth of July cannon. Ironically, the inventors and firers of the cannon received not so much as a scratch. Please, gentlemen, let's be more careful."

Off to this somewhat disturbing start, the marchers never did quite catch the rhythm of the drumbeat and fall into orderly ranks or step. But what they lacked in these departments was more than made up for by the volume of their singing. Caustic-tongued observers commented that no two people appeared to be singing in the same key, nor, for that matter, were they singing the same song. Even the uniformed fifer and drummer were out of step with each other, it was noted; as for Sumner Pinkham, he appeared to waddle rather than march, for he was far too patriotic a man to refuse any toast offered to the Union on such a great day, and he had many friends.

The best the watchers could make out, the drummer was beating time to *Battle Hymn of the Republic*, the fifer was tootling *Yankee Doodle*, and the crowd was just making noise—but there was no doubt in anybody's mind as to the song Old Pink was lustily singing:

"Oh, we'll hang Jeff Davis to a sour apple tree!
"Yes, we'll hang Jeff Davis . . ."

As the parade reached the center of town, where the crowds lining the boardwalks were denser, the booing, the heckling, the tripping, the shoving, became more active and intense. Here and there scuffles broke out; now and again blows severe enough to bloody noses and puff up lips were landed; an empty whiskey bottle tossed into the marchers' midst in a high, relatively harmless arc, came whizzing back with no visible hump in its line of flight, narrowly missed the head of a quietly smiling, perfectly innocent, politically neutral observer, struck the front window of a barber-and-bath shop owned by a Negro named Jack Johnson and shattered it utterly.

"Lawdy, Lawdy!" Johnson was heard to exclaim in dismay. "Look what comes from bein' free!"

Exactly what triggered the fuss between Ferd Patterson and Sumner Pinkham up at the head of the parade was never firmly established. It may have been the bully-boy crew of roughs who had been making a game of forming a human wedge and thrusting their way from one side of the street to the other through the marchers by brute force, thus destroying their unity. Tired of the sport, they persuaded Ferd Patterson to join their group, then he—with his customary brilliant thinking—suggested that the marchers now be split lengthwise, beginning with Old Pink himself, with Patterson leading the charge.

It may have been that sight of the yellow cur dog which some Democratic prankster had painted with red, white, and blue stripes, then tin-canned and tossed at Pinkham's feet, so offended the fervent Unionist that he swerved from his line of march and bumped into Patterson, this instigating the scuffle himself. Or it may simply have been, as was later claimed by many, that Ferd Patterson yelled out to Pinkham—who was still lustily singing—that if he didn't shut his mouth he'd shut it for him. Pinkham invited him to try, and he did.

In any event, there was a brief scuffle between the two men, the result of which was that Old Glory fell into the dust of the street. Some witnesses later swore they saw Ferd Patterson spit on it; others swore they heard Pinkham (who was unarmed at the moment) swear he would kill Patterson for that; others claim that the falling of the flag to the ground so shocked him that he said nothing, simply stooped, picked it up and then looked around for Patterson. But by then a swarm of men of both political parties—unwilling to see the flag of their country defiled—had separated the two men and warned the heckling roughs to let the patriotic parade proceed.

On one point, however, everyone agreed. Sooner or later a showdown must come between Old Pink and Ferd Patterson. When it did, blood would flow.

It happened one hot Sunday afternoon in late July . . .

The Warm Springs Resort a mile down Moore's Creek was a fine place to picnic, swim, drink, or steam out one's body poisons with a relaxed soaking in one of the number of private, zinc-lined, wooden tubs on either side of the long hall of the bathhouse. Strongly impregnated with sulphur and other health-restoring minerals, water heated far down in the bowels of the earth to a never-varying ninety degrees gushed out of a steep hillside to the west, filled a huge, wooden-lined, recently completed swimming pool in which properly attired gentlemen or ladies could paddle, play or float away all their aches. The water was conveniently available on tap in the individual bathrooms for those who preferred a private soaking in the raw.

Built on a slope, the front part of the resort had a long veranda bordered by a railing. To enter, a person had to climb several steps leading up from ground level to the veranda, walk its length, pass into the main room—which contained a bar—cross it, then go down the hall that led to the bathhouse section.

Sundays always were busy days. The resort-owned hack that plied between Warm Springs and Idaho City brought a new load of red-eyed, long-faced, unhappy-looking men every hour or so, who, as they got out of the conveyance and climbed the steps to the veranda appeared to be breathing their last. That the builder of the health spa had both an eye for profit and a keen knowledge of human frailty was evidenced by the fact that the room through which one had to pass to reach the baths—or, in busy times sit and wait—was amply stocked with the very poisons most of the customers had come to sweat out of their systems.

Badly hung over men preferred quiet, solitude and rest to crowds, activity and noise; thus, the suggestion when all the private bathrooms were occupied that the customer might like to get into bathing dress, climb the hill—which was steep—and take a swim in the outdoor pool until a private room became available, usually was greeted with a baleful stare and a profane suggestion as to what the host could do with his so-and-so swimming pool.

A drink, then, while you're waiting, Joe? Ha-ha! Nothing like a bit of hair off the dog that bit you, Joe! No, thanks. No, really. No—well, a small beer, maybe. And a jigger of whisky to give it some flavor. Did that help, Joe? Yeah, considerable. Sure, I'll have another. But skip the beer, this time; 'tain't good for a man to get too much liquid in his system . . .

Hey, boys, tell you what let's do—let's go for a swim! Last one up the hill's a monkey's uncle!

Both Ferd Patterson and Sumner Pinkham came to Warm Springs, that Sunday. Both were armed. Both had friends with them. Both took the waters in one manner or another, and each of them knew the other was there. Beyond these simple facts, later testimony of the many witnesses present finds no common ground of agreement.

Pinkham's friends claimed he tried to avoid a showdown. They said he was cold sober, did little if any drinking, and that he politely brushed Patterson aside as he was crossing the barroom on his way to a quiet private bath, saying, "That's all right, Patterson. We won't quarrel about it here."

Pinkham's friends further stated they are morally certain Ferd Patterson's sole purpose in coming to Warm Springs that day was to murder Pinkham, whom he secretly feared. They said Patterson's boasting had placed him so far out on a limb he had to kill Pinkham or become the laughingstock of his crowd; that, fearful of the results of a fair fight, he planned murder. He brought his friends along so that they might witness the foul deed, then protect his life afterwards by falsely swearing he killed in self-defense.

The Ferd Patterson partisans told it otherwise. They said Pinkham was the aggressor, that he called Patterson a name, that he drew first, that he fired first.

Ferd Patterson, it was testified, had just come out of the barroom onto the veranda. Pinkham was standing at the far end of the veranda, awaiting the hack. Both friendly and hostile witnesses agree that Patterson called out these words:

"Will you draw, you Abolitionist son-of-a-bitch?"

or

"Oh, you *will* draw, will you, you Abolitionist son-of-a-bitch!"

or

"Draw on *me*, will you, you Abolitionist son-of-a-bitch!"

. . . but opinions differ as to the order and inflexion of the words.

A pistol shot sounded. Sumner Pinkham staggered. A second shot was fired, a third, and—some witnesses swore—a fourth, though a later examination of the weapons of the two antagonists make that appear doubtful. At least one of the shots came from Pinkham's pistol, at least two from Patterson's.

Then Sumner Pinkham, ex-sheriff of Boise County, fervent Unionist, band leader, patriot, and prominent citizen, slumped to the floor of the veranda, dead . . .

Men being the fallible creatures they are, courts of law have long since learned to expect only a small portion of the full truth from even the most reliable of witnesses. A murder in cold blood or the eruption of passions into sudden action are totally different acts in the eyes of the law; but both acts happen the same way. Without warning. Without prologue. Without a referee's calling: "Come to time!"

A rider about to mount a horse hears a pistol shot ten paces away on a peaceful Sunday afternoon; and for minutes thereafter is too busy fighting his spooked mount to watch two men trying to kill each other. A purified bather sleepily gazing into the distance as he leans on a veranda railing is too interested in preserving his own life as bullets singe his coat-tail to recall afterward whether he stood dispassionately watching the gunfight and counting who fired how many times at whom or dived over the railing as any prudent man would do, then cravenly sought shelter under the porch, keeping his eyes closed all the while. Later, of course, he puts the best face possible on his reactions and swears *his* account is the *true* account.

But these things are known beyond doubt:

While Pinkham's stunned friends milled about uncertainly, Ferd Patterson's cronies hustled him away, mounted him on a saddle horse that may or may not have been brought along for exactly that purpose, and sent him galloping off—not toward Idaho City, but down-valley, toward Boise City. Word of the killing soon reached Sheriff Bowen, who set out in pursuit.

Minutes ahead of the sheriff and riding hard was Orlando Robbins, familiarly known as "Rube," a close personal friend of Sumner Pinkham, a former deputy under him, and a tough-minded, hard-fibered man. Some twenty miles down the trail, Robbins overtook Patterson, ordered him to give up his firearms, declaring he was making a "citizen's arrest." To Robbins' great disappointment (as he later confided to a friend), Ferd Patterson obeyed the order and surrendered "as meek as a lamb."

Minutes after the former deputy had disarmed the prisoner, Sheriff Bowen showed up and took him into custody. It well may be (as many Idaho citizens later claimed) that Sheriff Bowen was a .22-caliber man trying to hold down a .45-caliber job. But this much must be said for him—he got his prisoner back to Idaho City without a hand being laid on him. That was no small feat, considering the fact that a lynch mob of a thousand or so angry Unionists was determined to take him and hang him to the nearest tree despite anything the law and a large crowd of his friends might do to protect him.

Then, with Ferd Patterson secured behind bars, Sheriff Bowen quietly turned in his badge.

Deputy Sheriff Crutcher, unexpectedly elevated to the top law enforcement job, proved to be a man made of sterner stuff.

"The prisoner is mine," he declared. "I'm going to use every means at my disposal to preserve his life. If necessary, I'll throw a screen of riflemen around the jail and give them orders to shoot to kill. I'm deputizing every honorable man in Idaho City—"

"'Honorable men!' he says," howled a Unionist in the

crowd gathered in the street near the beleaguered jail. 'You know what he means, don't you, boys? Roughs! Scum! Secesh Democrats! Come on, fellas, what are we waiting for?'"

Well, what *are* we waiting for? A leader. A brave, strong man who'll tell us what to do. No, not *what*. On that, we're agreed; we simply want to take Ferd Patterson out of the jail and hang him. But *how* to accomplish this little chore without starting a second Civil War is the burning question.

Say the word, Rube Robbins. You ain't afraid of the devil himself; you were Old Pink's deputy; you were Old Pink's friend; you know the ways of violence. Ah, there's the rub! You're not a fool; you know if we storm the jail, some of us will die. And just because you yourself once wore a badge under the ablest peace officer the Territory has ever known, you've got a sneaking, grudging, reluctant smidgen of admiration for Jim Crutcher's guts in doing his duty as he sees it . . .

"Now, boys," Rube Robbins said, "let's not go off half-cocked. Now, boys, let's do some figuring . . ."

All right, goddam it, let's figure. Figure away the night, figure away the next day, figure, figure, and figure through the days and nights that follow. And all the figures add up to are a passel of damn-fool suggestions.

"What we need is a cannon!"

"Sure, Louie and Karl can make us one, like they done for the Fourth of July—"

"Oh, Lord, no! We don't want *that* kind of cannon!"

"Well, Paul and Johnny served in the Union Navy. They say they know how to make hand grenades. We'll get 'em to make us a batch, then we'll sneak up close to the jail and heave 'em—"

"Count me out on *that* idea, bully-boy! A rifle can throw lead a damn sight further'n a man can heave a grenade!"

"Hey, I got an idea! We'll ride down to Fort Boise and borrow a cannon—"

"The colonel won't loan us no cannon, you know that."

"We'll steal one, by God! We'll get some of them soldiers drunk . . ."

Well, now, there was an idea that just *might* work. Appoint a committee to ride to Boise City. Take up a collection to buy some whiskey. Dig deep, boys, it's for a worthy cause.

More meetings, more figuring. More procrastinating by the Democrat-dominated justice machine to keep the fires of indignation burning in the breasts of Old Pink's friends.

Ferd Patterson was being treated like no ordinary prisoner, it was said; instead, he was being wined, dined, and feted like a royal guest. The grand jury refused to bring an indictment against him. Judge Milton Kelly, a Democrat, congratulated Sheriff Crutcher and the hundreds of Democratic roughs he had deputized to guard the jail for their outstanding work in upholding law and order. The only reason that Patterson did not walk out of jail a free man, it was rumored, was that at the moment he felt safer inside its walls than out.

"He's damn sure right there!" an outraged Unionist declared. "Once he walks out of that jail, he's a dead man!"

The only cause for rejoicing that Pinkham's friends had during the next few days was the ruling by Federal Judge John McBride, who arrived in Idaho City two weeks after the killing, that a new grand jury must be impaneled. Nudged by his stern urging, this one did indict Patterson for murder in the first degree and the court set a date for his trial.

"Which doesn't mean he'll be convicted," a former Republican official pointed out. "Hell, we all know that the county sheriff picks the jury panel. He can pick a jury to acquit or convict, just as he likes. We know what Crutcher will do, don't we, boys?"

"Sure, we know! He's a Democrat, ain't he?"

"Here's something else to think about, boys. In the past three years, there have been sixty murders in the Boise Basin. *Sixty*, mind you! And how many murderers have been convicted and sentenced to hang? Not one! *Not one single solitary killer has ever paid the supreme penalty!* You can mark my word, boys, if we expect justice to be done, we've got to do it ourselves!"

By now, the delegation sent to Boise City to borrow or steal a cannon from the fort had returned with the sad report that their mission had been a failure. Hearing of what had happened, the Fort Boise commandant was being very careful

Idaho State Historical Society 5-B
The Idaho Territorial Penitentiary at Idaho City, circa 1860.

with his cannons, these days. Furthermore, he had seen fit to issue a stern warning that, in view of the fact that the Idaho City jail contained territorial as well as county prisoners, any mob attempt to take it by force very well might bring federal troops to its defense.

"If that don't frost the cake!" an angry Unionist cried in disgust. "Threatenin' us with United States government troops when all we want to do is hang a goddam Secessionist!"

Despite the growing pressure on him, Rube Robbins urged forbearance. But Sumner Pinkham had many friends. His funeral had been the largest, most impressive ever seen in that part of the world; and the sight of the immense number of mourners attending it had given men formerly reluctant to take the law into their own hands a knowledge of their strength. In spite of Democratic rumors to the contrary, no Vigilante Committee yet existed in the Boise Basin. Now, responsible men were openly suggesting that an organization of the righteous was the only way to clean up the country.

"Count me in," said John Gilkey, an amiable, normally placid-natured blacksmith from Buena Vista Bar. "Over in Virginia City, Montana, I hear, the roughs had things all their way till decent men hung Sheriff Henry Plummer and twenty-five of his cronies. Things have been peaceful there ever since. If that's the answer, let's get on with it."

Elder Kingsley, a highly respected Methodist minister, was asked his opinion. He made more converts for his church from one brief statement than he had ever made in a two-hour sermon, by saying, "Gentlemen, I'm prepared to fight or pray, as required."

It was then that Rube Robbins decided to act. "Boys, we seem agreed as to what needs to be done," he said quietly. "The question is how to do it. Sit tight till you hear from me. I'm going on a little trip."

"Where to, Rube?"

"Over to Horseshoe Bend to see Billy McConnell. Billy was Pink's friend, too. He'll know what to do."

Settling in the Payette River area just to the west of Idaho City a few years earlier, William J. McConnell had proved himself to be a strong supporter of law and order, despite his youth. When roving bands of horse thieves and bogus-gold-dust dealers became pests, he had helped organize a group of men called the Payette Valley Safety Committee. By threatening the roughs with banishment, whipping, or worse, the Safety Committee soon ended the crime wave in its part of the territory. (In time to come, McConnell would serve two years as deputy U.S. marshal in the Boise Basin, then still later as governor of Idaho from 1893 to 1896. His daughter, Mary, would marry a young attorney named William E. Borah, who would become a distinguished United States Senator).

After listening to Rube Robbins' explanation of the explosive situation in Idaho City, what Billy McConnell advised was caution. Yes, he would ride back to the Boise Basin with Rube and attend a secret mass meeting whose purpose would be to organize a Citizens Militia, a Boise Basin Vigilante Committee, a Public Law and Order Committee, or whatever name the people chose to call it. No, he would not lead it or play any role that might cause violence or bloodshed. Bad as the existing law enforcement might be, he said, it must be allowed to take its course.

His advice prevailed. For several days prior to the trial, battalions of armed men marched and countermarched, spied and counterspied, advanced, withdrew, and performed brilliant flanking maneuvers in and around Idaho City. The maneuvers were reported in great detail by pro and con newspaper writers eager to show off their skills as war correspondents. But since neither side fired the shot required to start the war, it petered out, the troops quit the field, and Ferd Patterson got his day in court.

As expected, he was acquitted. The *Idaho World*, whose editor was a Democrat, commented:

> "Mr. Patterson has had a fair and impartial trial."

The *Idaho Statesman*, whose editor was a Republican, said acidly:

> "Ferd Patterson has been acquitted, as expected. Idaho juries do not inquire whether a crime has been committed. All they ask is: 'Was it a fair fight?' If so, they cry: 'Not guilty! Bully for the boy with the glass eye!'"

But Ferd Patterson did not linger in the Boise Basin to read the reviews of his trial, for he had sensed something prophetic in the words of the late Sumner Pinkham's friend, Billy McConnell, who had said, "You may give Patterson his trial without hindrance. Since the evidence has been arranged to secure his acquittal, he can go forth into the world. But the world is not big enough to hide him."

Leaving Idaho City, Patterson moved 300 miles west to Walla Walla, where he worked as a professional gambler through the winter. He told a friend he intended to live more quietly. Not so much drinking and carousing. No more violence. Well, yes, there was a certain private policeman employed as a watchman by the local merchants who had bawled him out for being loud and boisterous the other night. That sort of talk he would take from nobody. He had written the man's name, Hugh Donahue, down in his little black book—and told him so. If the such-and-such ever crossed him again . . .

One February morning, slightly hung over, Patterson went into Richard Bogle's barbershop on the corner of Third and Main. Hanging his hat, coat, gun belt, and tie on a rack at the far side of the room, he stretched out in a chair to be shaved. With a hot towel over his face, he did not see the night watchman, Hugh Donahue, come into the shop by the same back entrance Patterson had used. For a time, Donahue stood warming himself by the potbellied stove, his hands behind his back. One of the hands held a pistol.

His shave finished, Patterson sat up to have his hair dressed. As he did so, Donahue rushed at him and cried, "You must kill me or I'll kill you!"

With his pistol only a foot or two from Patterson's face, Donahue fired. The shot caught Patterson in the right jaw. He exclaimed, "Oh, my God!" tumbled out of the chair, and sprang for the door. As he ran, Donahue fired twice more, hitting his target with the second ball, missing with the third. Patterson succeeded in getting out of the barbershop and into Welch's Saloon, next door. There, he sank to the floor. Donahue followed, discharging two more bullets into him as he lay helpless. Once sure he was dead, the night watchman gave up his pistol and surrendered to the law.

"He threatened me," was all he would say then and during his subsequent trial. "I was afraid."

Seven of the jurors believed in a broad interpretation of his self-defense plea and voted for acquittal. Five were narrow-minded and voted for conviction. Donahue was remanded to jail to await another trial. Due to a faulty lock, a careless deputy, or a bit of skulduggery by persons unknown, Hugh Donahue found his cell door left ajar one night, walked out, and departed for places unknown.

Some say his pockets were filled with Boise Basin gold. Some say the scalped mistress in Portland grew jealous and hired him to kill her former playmate. Some say the gold—if he had any—came from California friends of men Patterson had slain there.Whatever the true story was, the final verdict must be that Ferdinand J. Patterson went to glory like all gunfighters—by meeting a man with a faster draw.

4

RICHARD BOGLE
REFUGE FOR HIS RACE

Richard Bogle, the Negro barber who had just finished shaving Ferd Patterson before he was shot, deserves more than passing mention, for he was an important witness in the trial of Hugh Donahue, though his testimony probably was discounted because of his race. In time to come, he would shelter many colored people who passed through Walla Walla, where he lived out his long life as a man of property and a respected citizen. Regarding him, the regional historian W. D. Lyman wrote in 1901:

"Richard A. Bogle, proprietor of the tonsorial parlors at No. 3 Second Street, was born in the West Indian Islands, September 7, 1835. When about twelve years old, he emigrated to New York, and a year later, in company with one John Cogswell, he removed to Michigan, whence, after a brief residence, he and Mr. Cogswell crossed the plains to Oregon, arriving in the "land of promise" October 15, 1851. He stayed in Oregon three years, then moved to Yreka, California, where he learned the trade of a barber under a man named Nathan Ferber, for whom he worked for the ensuing three years. During the next three he was proprietor of a restaurant and barber shop in Deadwood, California, but he subsequently engaged in mining. Returning at length to Roseburg, Oregon, he resumed his trade, and until 1862 he maintained a shop there. In that year, however, he emigrated to Walla Walla, whence he made an extensive mining tour, visiting Florence, Elk City, and Oro Fino. Upon his return, he bought an interest in a barbershop, and has been engaged in that business unceasingly since, except for a brief period, during which he was in Oregon.

"Mr. Bogle has been quite successful financially and is interested in the Walla Walla Building and Loan Association, and other business enterprises. He resides in a very pleasant and comfortable home at 122 E. Poplar Street. In Salem, Oregon, in January, 1863, he married Miss A. Waldo, and they have become parents of eight children, five of whom are now living, namely: Arthur Belle Warren, now in the Sandwich Islands; Kate, wife of C. M. Duffy, Pullman, Washington; Porter, at St. Paul; and Waldo, with his father."

In another part of his *Illustrated History of Walla County,* W. D. Lyman elaborates on the violent, dangerous times Richard Bogle lived through as he tried to shelter and provide a refuge for members of his race. During this period, a group of self-styled "Vigilantes" was imposing its brand of justice on as mean and law-defying a class of men as ever existed in that part of the Pacific Northwest.

"The courts became powerless to cope with the evil doers," Lyman writes. "In 1864 the Vigilantes organized, and then came a reign of terror to the outlaws. It suddenly seemed as though nature had granted trees a new and startling fruit, for it became a common thing to see dead men's bodies dangling from limbs. In one month during the busy season thirty-two men were reported as having been mysteriously hanged. The common expression as men met on the streets in the morning was, 'Well, who did we have for breakfast today?'"

Under these circumstances, it behooved men of all races to behave themselves and to avoid associating with any person who flouted the law, lest they suffer Vigilante justice. Since he had come to the United States at the age of twelve and had managed to endure and become a respected member of society in a number of frontier communities, Richard Bogle certainly knew the rules of survival. Lyman writes:

> "In those days the citizens of the place made it rather hard for men of African descent. A Negro could not get a room at a hotel. He was not allowed to eat in a public dining room. He could not buy a cigar or a drink in a gin room without first taking off his hat and showing due reverence to the august vendor of the booze. Consequently, it was customary for Mr. Bogle, out of the kindness of his heart, to allow colored strangers who happened to be in town to occupy the rear of his shop, where they could keep warm and sometimes cook a meal."

Among the visitors Bogle sheltered in the spring of 1865 was a twenty-year-old, happy-go-lucky, likeable young man known to the sporting community he associated with as "Slim Jim." Because of his amiability and willingness to do whatever he was asked of him, he soon became a pet of the gamblers, jockeys, horsemen, and petty thieves of the area, who would rather steal than work.

The favored strong-arm method used by a pair of holdup men named Six-Toed Pete Parker and Booger Bart Billings was for Booger Bart to seize the victim from behind and pinion his arms, while Six-Toed Pete thrust the point of a long, sharp knife against the ambushed man's belly and threatened to open him up from gizzard to gullet if he did not hand over his valuables.

After being robbed one night in the alley behind Charley Roe's Saloon, an outraged victim, who had recognized his assailants, notified the law officer, Sheriff Luke Kimbrough, who caught the two thieves red-handed and lodged them in the local jail. Though not a very sturdy structure, the jail, which adjoined the courthouse in which the culprits would face the judge the next morning, certainly was solid enough to hold the two culprits till they came to trial.

But Booger Bart's older brother, Big Red Billings, was a prosperous saloon owner and gambler, accustomed to bailing his sibling out of trouble. Summoning Slim Jim to his saloon, he made him an offer he could not resist.

"That fool kid brother of mine has gotten himself in a fix again," Big Red said disgustedly. "So I want you to do me a little favor."

"Sure, Mister Billings," Slim Jim said obligingly. "I'll do anything you say."

"Here's twenty dollars. Go to the hardware store and buy a file, a hacksaw, a big screwdriver, a chisel, and a small crowbar. Pick up some sandwiches at the restaurant, put them all in a flour sack, and take it to the jail. When the jailer asks what you're carrying, give him a bottle of whiskey and my regards. He'll make you no trouble."

After asking the saloon owner to repeat the list of items he was supposed to buy and deliver to the jail so he could memorize it, Slim Jim accepted the bottle of whiskey and the twenty dollars Big Red Billings gave him, along with the added incentive:

"Promise me you'll never tell anyone who hired you to do this, Slim Jim, and I'll give you another twenty dollars. Will you do that?"

"You bet, Mr. Billings!" Slim Jim answered fervently, overwhelmed by the prospect of receiving what was to him the fortune of a lifetime. "You can depend on me!"

Stopping at the hardware store and the restaurant to make the required purchases, Slim Jim delivered them to the prisoners as he had been told to do, with no objection from the jailer. After reporting back to Big Red Billings that he had successfully completed his mission, Slim Jim was given a pat on the back and the promised twenty-dollar reward. He was warned again not to tell anyone who had paid him to deliver the sack. Then he returned to the back room of Richard Bogle's barber shop, where he went to bed and slept like the innocent he was.

Supplied with good tools and a jailer too drunk to realize or care what they were doing, the two prisoners, Six-Toed Pete Parker and Booger Bart Billings, sawed and pried their way out of jail, then used the two saddled horses left for them at the tie-rail to ride west to Wallula Landing, twenty-nine miles away. Sure that Sheriff Luke Kimbrough would not follow them there, they downed several drinks to celebrate their escape from the clutches of the law, then rolled into their blankets on the sandy beach, intending to take the morning boat downriver to Portland. Much to their surprise, they woke up to find Sheriff Kimbrough glaring down at them, pistol in his hand.

"Git up, boys! We're goin' back to Walla Walla."

Disturbed by the fact that the Vigilantes had taken over the administration of justice in his territory, Sheriff Kimbrough had decided to send a message that no prisoners could break out of his jail without suffering dire consequences. Getting a bit carried away with his own rhetoric, historian Lyman reported a scene he surely did not witness:

"Now, you fellows probably realize you're in a pretty bad fix," the sheriff said. "If you want to save your necks, you better 'fess up who gave you them tools."

"Slim Jim," was the response that came with perhaps more alacrity than magnanimity.

That afternoon, the sheriff appeared at Richard Bogle's barbershop. "I'm looking for a fellow named Slim Jim."

"That's me," responded Jim promptly.

"Well, I want you to come along with me."

Jim, without any sign of surprise or hesitation, took his belt containing his pistol and "Arkansas toothpick" and handed it to the barber, saying as he did so, "Here, Dick just keep these for me till I come back."

At the jail, he was confronted with the charge of having aided in the escape of the prisoners. He promptly confessed, pleading for his excuse that he "didn't know as it was so wrong."

"Well, I'll tell you just one way to save your neck," the sheriff said. "Tell me who put you up to this."

"I swore I wouldn't."

"That don't make no difference. If you want to save your skin, you've got to tell."

"When I make a promise, I ain't a-goin' back on it," Slim Jim said stubbornly. "You can shoot me or hang me or do anything else to me, but Slim Jim is a-goin' to stick to his word."

Though it was plain to see that the young Negro was very frightened, it was also clear to the sheriff and all the other men present that Slim Jim was not going to go back on his sworn promise. This so impressed several of them that they interceded in his behalf, finally persuading the sheriff to release him if he swore never to do such a thing again, which he did.

If he had been wise, Richard Bogle told historian Lyman when relating the story to him later, Slim Jim would have left town immediately. But he did not, staying in Walla Walla and enjoying a few drinks and a session of yarn-spinning with his sporting world friends, who admired him for not breaking his promise to the saloon keeper, Big Red Billings. Four nights after the jailbreak, Richard Bogle, as he prepared to close the barber shop and go home, told Slim Jim and several other men who were staying in the back room, that it would be a good idea to lock all the doors before they went to bed.

"Some of the stories going around town are making me nervous," he said. "Be sure and lock up good."

Though every resident of Walla Walla knew Richard Bogle by sight and no one had ever stopped him on the street before, that night he was challenged six times in four blocks by riders wearing coats with collars turned up and hats pulled down so that the only part of their face visible was their eyes.

"Halt!" a gruff voice cried out in the darkness.

When he did so, the rider moved his horse nearer, bent down, and peered intently at his face. "Who are you?"

"Dick Bogle, the barber, sir."

"What are you doing on the street at this hour?"

"Going home for a late supper, sir. Had a lot of customers today."

"All right, Dick. We're not after you. Just keep walking and don't look back.

Later, Bogle learned that there had been fifteen or sixteen

men sleeping on the floor in the back room of his barber shop between one and two o'clock in the morning. Having had a few nips out of the bottle Slim Jim had generously provided, they had been in a good mood when they finally turned in, neglecting to close and lock the back door, as he had cautioned them to do. Lyman writes:

"Suddenly down Main Street there stole twenty-five or thirty dark figures. Each was masked and each carried a rifle. They stopped in front of the barbershop. Half of them remained there while the rest went quietly around to the rear door. Silently they filed through the open door. They took their places at the feet of the sleeping Negroes, each vigilante covering a sleeper with his gun. Presently all the sleepers were aroused from their slumber by a rude voice.

"Whoever moves will have his head blown off."

Beside themselves with terror, the Negroes began to plead for mercy, but were summarily silenced.

"What's your name?" said the man who stood over the first Negro.

"Jones."

"We don't want you." To the next one. "What's your name?"

"Bill Davis."

"We don't want you."

The questioning continued until the night visitors got to the man they sought.

"What's your name?"

"Slim Jim."

"We want you. Put on your boots."

Jim obeyed slowly and deliberately, Lyman writes, then suddenly turned to his companions and exclaimed, "Boys, these fellows mean to kill me. Stand by me!"

Springing upon the man who stood over him, Slim Jim managed to wrench the rifle out of his hand, but because the men in the room were too paralyzed with fear to help him, his effort proved futile. Clubbed to the floor and knocked unconscious, he was dragged from the room and out into the night where his screams of protest soon dwindled away into the distance.

Again getting carried away by the drama of a scene he did not witness, historian Lyman invokes Shakespearean language when he has an Old Negro who supposedly *was* there declaim:

"The noise of battle hurtled through the air. Horses did neigh and dying men did moan, and ghosts did shriek and squeal about the street."

When Richard Bogle came to work the next morning, he viewed an appalling scene. Huddled together in a corner of the back room were fifteen or so men, bunched like a band of sheep chased by a dog.

"What's the matter?" he asked.

No one answered. Looking around the room, he saw streaks of blood on the floor and in the archway leading to the front of the shop.

"Come on, fellows, tell me what happened. Where's Jim?"

Without saying a word, one of the men finally got up, went to the door, and pointed down the street with a trembling hand. "Out there somewhere. They took him away."

Before long, the whole town knew that the body hanging from a stout limb of the old elm tree near Singleton's Pond on South Second Street, just two blocks from the city cemetery, was that of the amiable Negro boy, Slim Jim, who had done his last favor for a sporting world white friend.

Though the Vigilantes seem to have hanged Slim Jim because he had given aid and comfort to criminals, not because he was a Negro, people of color had to behave exceptionally well in order to get along in the overwhelmingly white world then existing in the Pacific Northwest. The fact that Richard Bogle succeeded says a great deal for the quality of his character. His story is one that should be told by the descendants of his family, many of whom still live in the Portland area today.

5

JOSEPHINE WOLFE
WALLA WALLA'S GENTEEL MADAM

If engaging in an illegal profession makes a person an "Outlaw," then Josephine Wolfe certainly was one, though she never carried a gun, held up anybody (in the normal sense of the term), or committed an act of violence in her life.

Josephine came to San Francisco from the Alsace region of Europe between Germany and France. A slim, dark-eyed beauty of sixteen, Josephine possessed such charm and talent as an "entertainer" in the fleshpots of the Barbary Coast that the professional gambler who owned the establishment married her, permitting her to retire from the practice of her trade and take over management of the bordello.

Though the record is murky, Josephine seems to have borne him a daughter, whom she determined to raise as a lady and a Catholic. Because she spoke English with a strong Teutonic accent, she became known in her later years as "Dutch Jo," though the nickname was seldom used in her presence.

When her husband was killed in a gunfight over a card game, Josephine sold her interest in the bordello for a substantial sum. She then took her seven-year-old daughter, a dozen of her girls, several male musicians, and her burly personal bodyguard north to the Pacific Northwest in search of business and a better environment in which to raise her child.

In those days, the usual mode of travel was by ocean-going steamship from San Francisco to the mouth of the Columbia, then up that river 100 miles to Portland, Oregon. There, if the travelers were going first-class, they would spend the night in a good hotel, then embark next morning in a smaller craft capable of negotiating the hazards upriver.

From Portland, shallow-draft side-wheelers chugged forty-five miles east to a set of rapids called the Lower Cascades, where the passengers took a narrow-gauge portage train six miles to the Upper Cascades. There, they went aboard another side-wheeler for the fifty-mile journey to The Dalles (French for "stepping stones"), passing through the awesome gorge which the Columbia River had carved though the 10,000-foot Cascade Range. Reaching the bustling metropolis of The Dalles on the "dry side" of the mountains in late afternoon, passengers who could afford it—as Josephine Wolfe certainly could—enjoyed the amenities of the Umatilla House, justly called "the finest hotel between Portland and St. Louis."

Next morning, the travelers rose at an early hour and took another portage train fourteen miles east to Deschutes Landing, upstream from Celilo Falls, where they resumed their trip aboard the newly-completed stern-wheeler the *Colonel Wright*. The boat was named for the Army officer who had led a brutal campaign against the Indians and brought peace to the inland region a few years earlier. The big stern-wheeler already had made several trips up the Columbia to the mouth of its principal tributary, the Snake, then continued 140 miles up that river to the boomtown of Lewiston, Idaho. In 1860, gold was discovered near Lewiston and thousands of prospectors flooded the region.

Nobody seemed concerned that the Idaho gold strikes were made on the Nez Perce Indian Reservation, where by treaty whites were forbidden to trespass without permission. A simple adjustment of reservation boundaries made room for the diggers and the necessary towns. Having heard that 10,000 gold-mad men were in the area, Josephine Wolfe hoped to take advantage of the opportunities being offered her as the first bordello operator on the scene.

Aboard the *Colonel Wright*, with Josephine Wolfe and her

Penrose Library, Whitman College
St. Louis Hotel, Walla Walla, Washington, May 1882.

entourage, was competition of a sort in the form of a stout German tavern owner named Hans Stohlhofen. Hans was accompanied by his wife, Marta, their three teenage sons, Fritz, Johann, and Wolfgang, along with six red-cheeked, flaxen-haired, healthy young female dancers, known in that place and time as "Hurdy-Gurdy Girls".

What Josephine Wolfe planned to do was rent an establishment in Lewiston, which would become a refined "entertainment parlor" offering all the services usually provided at such places—for a substantial price. Hans Stohlhofen planned to open a place in Orofino, forty miles to the east. There a hardworking prospector could buy a schooner of beer, a drink of whiskey, and a three-minute dance with an athletic female partner—for a more modest sum, since a dance was all a young lady was allowed to sell.

By contract before she left Germany, each girl agreed to work for one year, turning all her earnings over to the man who brought her to America. Under no circumstances could she have improper relations with the customer, no matter how much he offered to pay her. When her year was up, the girl would be given $1,000 in gold, help in finding a husband, or a ticket home.

When Hans Stohlhafen was asked if he might not have trouble making the woman-hungry miners behave after they got a few drinks in their system, he shook his head, took the wooden tool with which he opened beer kegs out of his pocket, and tapped it against an open palm.

"Das est mein bung-starter. If a customer makes trouble, it becomes mein bum-stopper."

Pulling into the sandy beach at Wallula Landing, in mid-afternoon, where the Columbia River made a wide turn to the north, the *Colonel Wright* was scheduled for a two-hour stop. The halt was just long enough to unload passengers and freight bound for Fort Walla Walla and the town of the same name twenty-nine miles to the east. But a messenger riding cross-country from the mouth of the Snake River eleven miles away brought the master of the boat, Captain Leonard White, a piece of bad news, which he reluctantly relayed to the passengers.

"We'll have to tie up here for the night, folks. The Snake is blocked with ice floes."

Since only a few chunks of ice could be seen floating on the surface of the Columbia here, Captain White had to explain to the puzzled passengers that every spring when the thaw came upriver, ice jams made the Snake between its mouth and Lewiston too dangerous to be navigated. The safe thing to do was lay by in a sheltered cove or landing until the worst of the floating ice had passed.

"How long will that take?" a passenger asked.

"A day or two. Hard to tell."

Because the passenger list included a hundred or so unattached men, it had not surprised Captain White that they were eyeing both groups of females just as closely as Josephine Wolfe and Hans Stolhofen were watching them. But he was surprised when one of the young bucks cried:

"Hear that, boys? We're gonna be stuck here overnight— maybe even longer. Why don't we throw a party?"

Well, why not? Certainly all the ingredients for a great party were aboard the boat: a bar, dancing girls, musicians, a sandy beach on which to take moonlight walks, lots of high-spirited, free-spending men lonely for companionship and fun.

As usually happened on steamboat day, a squad of bluecoats had ridden down from Fort Walla Walla to Wallula Landing to pick up the mail and escort any military travelers back to the post. Discovering there were pretty young women aboard, the soldiers weren't about to leave until the boat departed. Word of the women's presence had spread among the civilian population of Walla Walla, too, for the clerks, merchants, farmers, and ranchers who came to the landing to check new arrivals on the boat were equally disinclined to leave the scene until the boat and the ladies departed.

So far as Josephine Wolfe and Hans Stohlhoven were concerned, a party would be good advertising for the businesses they were about to establish upriver—so long as proper decorum was observed. Even Captain White was not averse to a bit of music and fun, so long as drinks dispersed by the boat's bar were paid for and the men minded their manners.

According to local legend, the remaining daylight hours were spent decorating the boat's dining saloon with hanging lanterns and strings of ribbons. The musical talent aboard was inventoried and put under the baton of the silver-haired leader of the Josephine Wolfe ensemble. He played the piano beautifully and had brought a small one in the cargo hold. Under his direction, an orchestra was put together, with Fritz, Johann, and Wolfgang playing the tuba, clarinet, and accordion, while the bordello musicians and the bodyguard filled in on the coronet, cello, tambourine, fife, and drums. An hour's rehearsal proved the group capable of producing music for dancing—from waltzes to hoedowns—or music for singing—from *Annie Laurie* to *My Mother's Grave*. When the party began at dusk, the orchestra made music the likes of which the desert air of the river-bend country had never heard before.

Urged on by members of her entourage, who remembered what a dancing sensation she had been on the Barbary Coast as a sixteen-year-old beauty, Josephine Wolfe performed a passion-filled gypsy number which drove the men in the audience wild. Hans Stohlhofen put on a Falstaff act that made the crowd roar with laughter. The silver-haired piano player donned a wig, stuck a cigar in his mouth, and gave an imitation of Mark Twain—the most popular gold-camp entertainer of the day—lecturing a Ladies Club on the foibles of Modern Literature that was truly a riot.

Brought to a reluctant end at midnight, the party was pronounced a smashing success by all. Abiding by the ground rules laid down by Captain White, neither Josephine Wolfe's young ladies nor Hans Stohlhofen's hurdy-gurdy girls charged for whatever services they may have provided their partners. Because they were all adults and fallibly human, no guarantees were made as to what may or may not have happened during moonlit strolls along the sandy beach.

Inevitably, there were consequences. At noon next day, two of Josephine Wolfe's girls told her they were leaving her employment. One of them had met and fallen in love with a Walla Walla businessman. The other had been smitten by a local rancher. Josephine Wolfe asked them just one question:

"Will they marry you?"

"Oh, yes!" the girls exclaimed in unison. "We made them promise to take us to a preacher before we will go home with them."

"Then you have my blessing, dears. But you know my rules. You cannot work for me again."

None of Hans Stohlhofen's girls had accepted offers of marriage made them by lonely local swains, for the price he asked was far too high. Estimating the fees he would receive for the services of each girl during the course of the year she had agreed to work for him at $5,000, Hans insisted on receiving that sum before he released her from her obligation. Furthermore, if she left him before her year was up, he would give her neither the $1,000 nor the ticket home. This was a penalty neither the girls nor their suitors were prepared to pay.

When Captain White learned that ice floes still choked the Snake and told the passengers that the *Colonel Wright* would have to lay over at the landing for another night, the cry for "another party" immediately was raised by the jubilant men, whose numbers were increasing hourly as the news spread. Josephine Wolfe and Hans Stohlhofen were dismayed.

Already she had lost two of her best girls, Josephine Wolfe told Captain White, while Hans Stohlhofen said that if the boat stayed here much longer he feared one or more of his girls would leave him, despite the stiff penalties. "Can't we at least go up the river a few miles?" he begged. "These lovesick men are driving my girls crazy."

"I suppose we could go up to the Snake and pull into a cove called Ice Harbor," Captain White said thoughtfully. "I doubt if the men will follow us there."

"Do it, please," Josephine Wolfe pleaded. "I can't afford to lose any more girls."

The *Colonel Wright* steamed eleven miles north up the flood-swollen Columbia, then ten miles east up the ice-choked Snake to seek refuge in a bluff-surrounded cove on the south shore to which there were no trails or roads. But according to local legend the boat only beat the pursuing crowd of bachelors by a half an hour. As the whooping, boisterous column of men came riding recklessly down the face of the steep lava bluff, they were shouting:

"A party! We want another party!"

Legend relates that during the two days the *Colonel Wright* laid by in Ice Harbor waiting for the floes to pass, Josephine Wolfe lost two more girls, while Hans Stohlhofen lost one. Their names are unknown, of course, for latter-day emigrant societies record only the names of what then were called "Honorable Women." But in time to come, most of them would lead respectable lives and become the mothers and grandmothers of some of the best citizens of the region.

Though Hans Stohlhofen established a successful and profitable business in Orofino, Josephine Wolfe did not stay long in Lewiston. She found the town too crude and raw for her tastes. She returned to Wallula Landing, then moved inland to the older town of Walla Walla. There she rented the entire second floor of a new brick building and furnished an "Entertainment Parlor." As a supply center for the mines, a wintering place for prospectors who had struck it rich, a farming, ranching, and transportation community, with a good Catholic school and church, Walla Walla was exactly the kind of city Josephine was looking for. Here, she would spend the rest of her long life, becoming known as "Dutch Jo."

Because she shunned publicity and her name seldom appeared in print, almost all the information I have gathered about Dutch Jo has come from descendants of people who knew her. Very few of them would permit me to quote them directly, so I have lumped all their stories and the bits and pieces of material found in early-day newspapers and history books, which I feel refer to her in an oblique way, as "the legend of Dutch Jo." Which is just another way of saying I believe the stories are true, though I can't prove it.

If she did have a seven-year-old daughter whom she wanted to enroll in a good Catholic school, the child's name was never recorded. Since no daughter is mentioned in her will, a copy of which I have seen, I suspect the daughter either died or did not exist.

Certainly Dutch Jo was a strong supporter of the Catholic Church and extremely generous in her contributions to it and the charitable causes it sponsored. In her way, she was a very moral woman, with strict rules regarding the girls who worked for her. The first rule was that she would never start a girl in the trade, employing only young ladies who had gotten into the profession of their own volition. The second was that the girls could leave her for any reason at any time they wished. If they did, however, they must not stay in town unless they got married and embarked on what the world called a "respectable" life.

On one occasion, so the story goes, two sixteen-year girls from a nearby town became enchanted with the beautiful clothes and rich life style apparently enjoyed by Dutch Jo's girls. They lied to her about their ages, experience, and identities, claiming they had worked at the trade in Portland and had come upriver to Walla Walla because they heard that the pay and working conditions were better.

After listening sympathetically to their fabricated story, Dutch Jo assigned each of them to a room, told them to rest and freshen up, and to expect male visitors to come presently and check out their talents. And presently male visitors did come—the girls' fathers, whom Dutch Jo knew well and had summoned.

She had a reputation for treating the young delivery boys who brought newspapers and groceries very well, often giving them a five-dollar gold piece as a Christmas bonus. On one occasion, a twelve-year-old boy proudly showed his mother the coin Josephine Wolfe had given him, bragging, "It's even got her initials scratched on it—'J. B'."

Bill Gulick

Josephine Wolfe Monument
Walla Walla Cemetery

"But, dear," his mother said, "her initials are 'J. W.' You must have made a mistake and read it wrong."

The son had made a mistake, the mother saw after taking the coin and studying it closely. The initials were "J. B."—her husband's, scratched on the coin in his distinctive style of lettering.

Of course there was a possibility that the boy's father could have gotten the gold coin in a perfectly innocent sort of way. During the boom years in Walla Walla, at least four entertainment parlors existed, all of them discreetly located in a two-block area west of 2nd and Main. Nightly, a city policeman paid each house a call, making sure that no unruly behavior was taking place or expected, receiving as a reward for his courtesy a drink, a cigar, and two silver dollars. So if a customer did misbehave, the law was quickly enforced.

Because all the houses were good customers and paid their

bills weekly in cash, many of the merchants, city officials, and charitable-contribution-seekers got in the habit of "making the rounds" each Friday afternoon, enjoying a social session at each house before presenting their bills. Beginning at 4 p.m. and continuing until 6 p.m., the delegation traveled in a body, beginning with a visit to the least pretentious establishment, then moving up the scale to Dutch Jo's, where they were assured of the finest drinks, eats, entertainment, and hospitality. In this particular part of the country, thunder and lightning storms rarely occurred. But if a bolt of lightning had happened to strike the second floor of the building Dutch's Jo's entertainment parlor occupied at 5:30 on a Friday afternoon, it would have scorched a goodly segment of the town's leading citizens.

According to local legend, lightning of a kind did strike one Friday afternoon when Dutch Jo asked a visiting doctor, who was also the city health officer, to examine one of her girls, whose face had broken in a rash. He announced that the girl had scarlet fever and quarantined the house for two weeks. None of the people present were permitted to leave. The list of detainees included the mayor, fire chief, police chief, a Catholic priest, an Episcopalian minister, a newspaper publisher, and six merchants.

For the next two weeks, so the story goes, much of the town's business was conducted by means of a basket lowered and raised from a second-story window, being fumigated at each end of the trip.

At some time before her death, Dutch Jo bought a lot in the city cemetery for herself and several adjoining lots for those of her girls who had expressed a wish to lie beside her. By the time she died in 1909, at the age of seventy-three, she had become a wealthy woman, owning several hundred acres of fertile wheat land outside the city and considerable valuable business property in town.

Her will sheds little light on her life, though it does raise some interesting questions. Since she had no known relatives, she distributed her money among her friends and her church. But why did she will a parrot named "Hot Lake" to the owner of the most successful jewelry store in town? Why did she leave $5,000 to "our heroic firemen?" Why did she offer only ten dollars "to anyone who can prove they are related to me. . . ?" Why did she order all pictures and portraits of herself destroyed upon her death?

No one knows. But she is part of Walla Walla's colorful pioneer past.

6

HENRY PLUMMER
OUTLAW SHERIFF OF ALDER GULCH

Following the discovery of gold in California in the late 1840s, other strikes were made through the 1850s and '60s in the mountains of Nevada, Oregon, and what would soon become the territories of Washington, Idaho, and Montana.

Because the prospectors who made the first strikes were honest, hard-working men, there was little crime in the camps at first, where simple wilderness courtesy required that no doors be locked and that a wandering stranger could help himself to whatever food and fuel he found if he were hungry and cold. The unwritten law was that the visitor chop a new supply of firewood, leave the cabin as clean and animal-proof as he had found it, and repay its owner for any food or supplies he used during his stay, if and when his fortunes improved.

But the second wave of newcomers was a different breed of men. Digging for gold was hard, back-breaking work, for which most of them had a strong aversion. They used their smooth, soft hands for dealing cards or rolling dice and their quick wits for acquiring wealth by means that required no heavy lifting. Before law and order came to the camps, the thieves, the gamblers, and a class of men called "roughs" not only bullied, robbed, and killed honest, industrious citizens, but actually got some of their own kind elected to positions of authority.

Such a man was Henry Plummer.

Though Montana newspaper editor Thomas Dimsdale says that more than twenty contradictory accounts of Plummer's early years were "recommended" to him, he believes the man came originally from Boston to Wisconsin, then to Nevada City, California, in 1853. There he opened the Empire Bakery in partnership with a man named Henry Hyer. This apparently was the only legitimate business enterprise Plummer ever engaged in. According to Dimsdale, everyone who came in contact with him agreed that:

"Plummer was a man of most insinuating address and gentlemanly manners under ordinary circumstances, and had the art of ingratiating himself with men and even with ladies and women of all conditions. Wherever he dwelt, victims and mistresses of this wily seducer were to be found. It was only when excited by passion that his savage instincts got the better of him and that he appeared—in his true colors—a very demon. In 1856 or 1857 he was elected marshal of the city of Nevada, and had many enthusiastic friends. He was re-elected and received the nomination of the Democratic Party for the assembly near the close of his term of office; but as he raised a great commotion by his boisterous demeanor, caused by his success, they 'threw off on him,' and elected another man."

If the style and quality of the writing make the frontier newspaper editor sound like an unusually well-educated man for his place and time, he certainly was. Born and raised in England and an Oxford graduate, Thomas H. Dimsdale emigrated to Canada as a relatively young man, contracted "consumption," and moved to the mountains of Montana in the summer of 1863, hoping that the pure, fresh air would improve his health.

During the winter of 1863-64, he taught in a private school, charging each pupil two dollars a week, conducting a singing school on the side. A man of culture and refinement, he drew to himself all that was best of the society of that time in Virginia City and is described as "a gentle, kind-hearted Christian man."

Organized as Montana Territory on May 26, 1864, with Bannack as its temporary capital, the region was settled by prospectors who had followed first the gold and then the silver veins north from California and Nevada. Too busy searching for precious metals to be original or to spell correctly, the miners chose "Bannack," "Nevada," and "Virginia City" as names for the new settlements, ignoring the confusion caused the post office over the fact that similarly-named towns already existed in other states or territories.

As a matter of fact, the Nevada gold-boom town finally named "Virginia City" originally was called "Varina" in honor of the wife of Confederacy President Jefferson Davis. But with the Civil War raging and Union supporters in control of the postal service, *that* name was not going to get past the postmaster; so "Virginia" was substituted.

The first and what would prove to be the biggest strike in the area was made in Alder Gulch, with an estimated $100 million in gold being recovered from the vein before it was worked out. Soon after Montana Territory was organized, Governor Edgerton appointed Thomas Dimsdale its first superintendent of schools. He also became the editor of the *Montana Post*, the first newspaper of consequence in the area, thus was in an ideal position to observe and report the violent events that followed during the Henry Plummer period.

As an observer and recorder of Henry Plummer's career, Dimsdale cannot be faulted for his writings, even though they at times seem verbose, flowery, and laced with moralizing, in the style of the day.

Henry Plummer's first recorded act of violence occurred when he killed a German named Vedder, with whose wife he was having an affair. For this offense, Plummer was arrested and tried, first in Nevada, where he was convicted and sentenced to two years in prison; and second, in Yuba County, on a rehearing with a change in venue. Here the verdict was confirmed and he was sent to prison.

Here, too, his faculty for persuading friends in high places to intercede in his behalf served him well. Alleging that he was so seriously ill with a "consumptive" disease that a long prison stay would kill him, his friends not only secured Plummer's release after a few months' incarceration, but also persuaded Governor John P. Weiler to give him a full pardon. Returning to Nevada City, Plummer resumed his partnership with Henry Hyer, their enterprise now being called the Lafayette Bakery.

But the selling of baked goods did not interest Plummer nearly as much as fraud and violence. During the next few years, he got involved in one scrape after another, some of them ludicrous in their execution and outcome. First, he concocted a plan by which a friend named Thompson, who was more popular locally now than he was, would run for the office of city marshal, then, after getting elected, would resign in favor of Henry Plummer. Unfortunately, the two conspirators downed a few too many drinks before Election Day, bragged about their scheme in the hearing of too many voters, and the "stalking horse" candidate lost.

A short while later, Plummer got into an argument with a friend while visiting a house of ill fame, struck him over the head with a pistol, and was held on charges of attempted murder until the friend regained consciousness. To show that there were no hard feelings between them, Plummer and the friend strolled arm in arm around town for several days. The charges were dropped.

Bored with inactivity, Plummer went over to the nearby town of Washoe and joined a band of road agents who were planning to hold up a Wells Fargo gold shipment. In an attempt to carry out his role as stick-up man, Henry Plummer drew his revolver and leveled it at the driver of the stagecoach. But because he had neglected to insert the metal key which held the barrel and stock together, the barrel fell off, rendering the revolver inoperative. Observing this, the driver of the bullion express laughed, lashed his horses into a run, and the robbery failed.

So did the ensuing trial, in which Plummer was acquitted for "lack of evidence."

A few months later, the "friend" Plummer had beaten unconscious in the brothel brawl died from head injuries. The examining doctor said the death was the result of the earlier pistol-whipping. Since the charges for the original beating had been dropped, no new ones could be filed.

Plummer's final "difficulty" in Nevada City occurred while he was living with a mistress in a local brothel. During a quarrel with a man named Ryder, who also had a female companion sleeping under the same roof, guns were drawn, shots exchanged, and Ryder fell dead. Jailed and charged with murder, Plummer found friends and funds with which to bribe the jailer to let him escape. Deciding to seek new and perhaps healthier fields to conquer, Plummer headed north for Washington Territory.

Somewhere along the way, Plummer concocted the brilliant scheme of discouraging pursuit by writing a letter to a widely-read San Francisco newspaper stating that, after committing a murder in Washington Territory, "the notorious outlaw, Henry Plummer, was taken by a local Vigilante Committee and hanged." He of course signed the letter with a fictitious name.

While he did not add the footnote: "Nevada papers please copy," he had little doubt that they would do exactly that, which would tend to close his case.

How prophetic that spurious letter would be did not occur to Henry Plummer at the time. During his brief stay in Washington Territory, he seduced a man's wife in Walla Walla, stole a horse, and then joined a rough named Cherokee Bob, who had just killed a soldier in a gunfight in a local theater, in a midnight flight to Lewiston and the interior gold-boom towns of Idaho and Montana.

Some historians claim that Plummer's brief stay in Walla Walla was caused by that city's decision to end the local crime wave by making a number of citizen arrests, conducting a few late-night peoples' court trials, and handing out a number of "suspended" sentences which were promptly executed under the stout horizontal limb of a stately elm tree on South Second Street, just a convenient half-mile north of the city cemetery.

After short visits to Lewiston and Orofino, Plummer moved on east to the gold camps where most of the action was taking place at that time—Bannack, Nevada, and Virginia City—arriving there late in 1862. Though he probably had little interest in geography or history, his trip took him across the Continental Divide to the headwaters of the Beaverhead, where on August 12, 1805, Hugh MacNeal, a member of the Lewis and Clark party, exulted that he had lived long enough "to stand astride the mighty Missouri River."

In this same area during the next two years, Henry Plummer made a different kind of history as "Chief" of a band of outlaws that, according to Thomas Dimsdale, murdered at least 102 men before being forced to pay for their crimes. Plummer organized the men into an efficient company of road agents and informers that identified every traveler along the seventy-five miles of east-west mountain trails between Bannack and Virginia City and the hundreds of miles of north-south wagon and stagecoach roads to Salt Lake City, Utah, and Butte, Montana. The gang members placed special markings on persons, pack animals, and vehicles carrying shipments of gold bullion so that their people would know who to rob. At the same time, members of their own gang were identified by having each individual wear a certain color of neckerchief knotted in a certain way, so that a fellow member could recognize him on sight. In what may have been only a slightly exaggerated description of the typical gang member, Dimsdale wrote:

> "The usual arms of a road agent were a pair of revolvers, a double-barreled shotgun of large bore, with the barrels cut down short, and to this they invariably added a knife or dagger. Thus armed and mounted on fleet, well-trained horses, and being disguised with blankets and masks, the robbers awaited their prey in ambush. When near enough, they sprang out on a keen run with level shotguns, and usually gave the word, 'Halt!

Throw up your hands, you sons of b-----s!' If this latter command were not instantly obeyed, that was the last of the offender."

Plummer's first recorded dispute occurred in the fall of 1862 when he and Jack Cleveland, an old acquaintance and former partner in crime, planned to spend the winter at Sun River Farm. When a young lady got involved in the arrangement the two men agreed Plummer would take care of the chores around the house while Cleveland went into the hills and chopped wood. Neither task got done because the partners did not trust each other out of sight.

Dimsdale says that Plummer later married the young lady, but she is mentioned no more, so she must have got lost along the way to Bannack. Their quarrel over her caused lingering ill feelings, however, for when he got a few drinks under his belt—which was often—Jack Cleveland swore that Henry Plummer was "his meat," while Plummer made similar statements of animosity toward his former associate in crime.

Though the two men had been strapped for funds when they arrived in Bannack, they both started spending money freely soon after they got there, their newly acquired prosperity coinciding with the robbery and murder of several local citizens. Then in Goodrich's Saloon one cold February day, the long-threatened "falling-out among thieves" occurred when Jack Cleveland declared, ""I'm a chief! I know all the rascals around here—and I'm going to get even with them!"

In reply to this statement, Plummer jumped to his feet, saying: "You d---d son of a b----h, I am tired of this!" Drawing his pistol, Plummer commenced firing at Cleveland.

The first ball lodged in the beam overhead; the second struck Cleveland below the belt. He fell to his knees, grasping wildly at his pistol, exclaiming, "Plummer, you won't shoot me when I'm down?"

"No, I won't!" Plummer replied. "Get up!"

As Cleveland staggered to his feet, Plummer shot him a little above the heart, the bullet, glancing on the rib and going around his body. The next slug entered below Cleveland's right eye and lodged in his head. The last bullet went between two men sitting on a nearby bench, who, to nobody's surprise, soon discovered that business called them elsewhere immediately.

Following the custom of the day, the town's one and only barber had set up his chair near the stove toward the back of the saloon.

"Singular enough it must appear to the inhabitants of settled communities," Dimsdale writes apologetically, "that a man was being shaved in the saloon at the time and, neither he nor the operator left off business."

Even more singular was the fact that when two of Henry Plummer's gang member friends, George Ives and Charley Reeves, heard he had been involved in a shooting, they rushed to the saloon with drawn pistols to protect him. They took him by the arm and escorted him out and down the street, their first concern being, "Will the d----d strangling sons of b------s hang you now?"

This is the first indication that local sentiment favoring some sort of justice was beginning to form. Representing the Law and Order group, a quiet-spoken, tough-fibered man named Hank Crawford had recently been asked to act as town marshal. Nursing a cold while boarding with a Bannack friend, I. W. Davenport, Crawford got out of his sick-bed when told of the shooting, bundled up, and went to the Goodrich Saloon to investigate. There, he found bystanders who had observed the fracas so fearful of Plummer and his gang that none of them had even dared to lift the head of the badly wounded man.

"We can't let him just lay there," Crawford said indignantly. "Is there no one that will take him home?"

Apparently no one would, for not a person present offered to do so. Though just a boarder himself, Hank Crawford said he would take Cleveland to his room in the Davenport house. Persuading three of the bystanders to help him carry the wounded man there, Crawford then sent for the doctor.

Beyond medical help, Jack Cleveland lingered for three pain-filled hours. Going to the rooming house in which both Cleveland and Plummer lived to pick up some blankets,

Hank Crawford encountered Henry Plummer, who arrogantly demanded,

"Is Jack still alive?"

"Yes. But he's not going to last much longer."

"What has he told you about me?"

"Nothing."

"It's well for him," Plummer said coldly, "or I would have killed the d---d son of a b---h in his bed."

Knowing it would be dangerous to argue with Henry Plummer at this place and time, Hank Crawford said that he must return to Jack Cleveland's bedside, took the blankets back to the boarding house, and resumed the death-watch. After Cleveland died, Hank Crawford saw to it that he was decently buried. But from that moment on, he told his Law and Order friends, he knew that he was a marked man so far as Plummer was concerned.

"He knows if Jack Cleveland talked, we have all the evidence we need to hang him."

"If we decide to do any hanging," a friend said skeptically, "Henry Plummer probably will top the list. But who's gonna start the ball rolling?"

At the moment, no one wanted to initiate Vigilante action, the general attitude being that so long as the shooting was contained among the roughs themselves, no harm was being done to law-abiding citizens. To a degree, this was true, for when gang members started shooting at one another, they often were so drunk and their aim so bad that their bullets did no damage. Typical of their brawls as reported by Dimsdale was a "shooting scrape" between George Carrhart and George Ives during the winter of '62-'63:

"The two men were talking together in the street close to Carrhart's cabin. Gradually they seemed to grow angry, and parted, Ives exclaiming aloud, 'You d---d son of a b----h, I'll shoot you,' and ran into a grocery store for his revolver. Carrhart stepped into his cabin and came out first with his pistol in his hand, which he held at his side. George Ives came out, and turning his back on

Carrhart, looked for him in the wrong direction, giving his antagonist a chance of shooting him in the back if he desired to do so. Carrhart stood still till Ives turned, watching him closely. The instant Ives saw him he swore an oath, and raising his pistol, let drive, but missed him by an inch or so, the bullet striking the wall of the house close to which he was standing. Carrhart's first shot was a misfire, and a second shot from Ives struck the ground. Carrhart's second shot flashed right in Ives' face but did no damage, though the ball could hardly have missed more than a hair's breadth. Carrhart jumped into the house, and reaching his hand out, fired at his opponent. In the same fashion his antagonist returned the compliment. This was continued until Ives' revolver was emptied—Carrhart having one shot left. As Ives walked off to make his escape Carrhart shot him in the back near the side. The ball went through, and striking the ground in front of him, knocked up the dust ahead of him. Ives was not to be killed by such a shot and wanted to get another revolver, but Carrhart ran off down the street. Ives cursed him for a coward 'shooting a man in the back.' They soon made up their quarrels, and Ives went and lived with Carrhart on his ranch for the rest of the winter."

Unfortunately, their chances for living happily ever after were considerably shortened when the senseless massacre of a group of innocent Indians by gang members so angered the community that the Law and Order people finally took action. Dimsdale noted sarcastically:

"If the facts here stated do not justify the formation of a vigilance committee, then may God help Uncle Sam's nephews when they venture west of the river in search of new diggings. In March, 1863, Charley Reeves bought a Sheep-Eater squaw; but she refused to live with him, alleging that she was ill-treated, and went back to her tribe, who were encamped on the rise of the hill south of

Yankee Flat, about fifty yards to the rear of the street. Reeves went after her and sought to have her come back with him, but on his attempting to use violence, an old chief interfered. The two grappled. Reeves, with a sudden effort, broke from him, striking him a blow with his pistol, and in the scuffle one barrel was harmlessly discharged."

Despite the fact that no damage had been done, Charley Reeves and a friend named Bill Moore reacted as if a dastardly sneak attack had been made upon the white race by a hostile Indian tribe. In an "advanced state of intoxication," next evening, the two men entered Goodrich's Saloon, laid a double-barreled shotgun and four revolvers on the bar, and made a drunken declaration of war.

If the d---d cowardly white folks were afraid of the Indians, they were not, they proclaimed, and soon would "set the ball rolling." Failing to enlist any volunteers to help them, they proceeded on their own, carrying their arsenal of weapons to a spot opposite the peaceful Indian camp, leveling their guns, and firing into the cluster of tepees.

After wounding one Indian with their first volley, they returned to the saloon, downed three more drinks apiece, and boasted of what they had done. Reinforced now by a man named William Mitchell and two other glory-hunters, they returned to the spot overlooking the Indian camp and opened fire again, this time with murderous effect. Dimsdale writes:

"Mitchell, whose gun was loaded with an ounce ball and a charge of buckshot, killed a Frenchman named Brissette, who had run up to ascertain the cause of the first firing—the ball striking him in the forehead, and the buckshot wounding him in ten different places. The Indian chief, a lame Indian boy, and a papoose were also killed; but the number of the parties who were wounded has never been ascertained. John Burne escaped with a broken thumb, and a man named Woods was shot in the groin, of which wound he has not yet entirely recovered.

This unfortunate pair, like Brissette, had come to see the cause of the shooting and of the yells of the savages. The murderers being told that they had killed white men, Moore replied with great sang froid, 'The d---d sons of b-----s had no business there.'"

Most of the general population disagreed and expressed their anger vocally. Alarmed by the indignation aroused and expressed in a mass meeting held the following morning, Bill Moore, Charley Reeves, and Henry Plummer thought it prudent to leave Bannack, fleeing to the gang's Rattlesnake Ranch headquarters a few miles from town. The thoroughly aroused Law and Order people were so incensed by the recent violence that they posted a ring of sentries around Bannack to prevent further egress, then called for volunteers to pursue the fleeing criminals and bring them back for trial. Aided by bitterly cold weather for which the fugitives were ill prepared, the accused men were soon captured, brought back, and charged.

Because there was no organized government in the area, the first question to be decided was whether the prisoners should be tried by the people *en masse* or by a selected jury. Some leading men favored the first method, Dimsdale says, while others felt a trial by jury would be best. Notable among the latter group was a thirty-year-old man named Langford, a person who in time to come would play such an important role in Montana history that a brief biographical sketch is given to him here.

Born in Oneida, New York, in 1832, Nathaniel Pitt Langford entered the banking business in St. Paul, Minnesota, in 1853. In 1862, he joined a party headed west for the Idaho gold fields. Arriving in the Bannack area shortly after the first strike was made there, he changed his plans, settling first near Bannack, then, a year later, moving to Virginia City, where he became a member of the Vigilante executive committee that later passed judgment on the Plummer Gang.

Though many of the Vigilantes were his friends, Langford refused to name most of them when he wrote his book *Vigilante Days and Ways*, even though it was not published until 1890, thirty years later. In 1864, he was named Collector of Internal Revenue for Montana, holding that position until 1868. He was a member of the 1870 Washburn Yellowstone Expedition, wrote a book about it, and worked for the establishment of Yellowstone National Park. After the park was created, he became its first superintendent, holding that position from 1872 to 1877.

Substantial citizen though he would become, his firm stand in favor of the Law and Order contingent put his immediate future in serious jeopardy. Dimsdale writes:

> "The assembly of citizens numbered about five or six hundred. After several hours' discussion a jury was ordered and the trial proceeded. At the conclusion of the evidence and argument the case was given to the jury without any charge. The Judge also informed them that if they found the prisoners guilty, they must sentence them."

Because no record of the proceedings was made, Dimsdale's rather disjointed report as to whom was charged, acquitted, convicted, or sentenced is difficult to follow. Apparently, the first charge was brought against Henry Plummer, who was accused of killing Jack Cleveland a few weeks earlier. Since it was common knowledge that bad blood long had existed between the two men, that Cleveland had threatened Plummer, and that Cleveland had a gun in his hand during the fight in Goodrich's Saloon, Plummer's plea of self-defense gained him a quick acquittal.

Next to be tried were Mitchell, Reeves, and Moore, whose drunken shooting into the Indian village certainly had no justification. The evening before the trial, a man named Rheem, who claimed to be an attorney, had promised to act as prosecutor, while an alleged "Judge" Smith would speak for the defense. But soon after a lawyer from St. Paul named

Hoyt was elected judge of the court and Hank Crawford was elected sheriff, Rheem announced that he had been hired by the defense, thus was switching sides, replacing Smith, who is heard from no more. Named as prosecutor now was a Mr. Copley, whose talents, according to Dimsdale, "did not lye in that direction, he was not successful as an advocate"

There is no indication of the direction of the talents of Defense Attorney Rheem, who could only plead that his clients were so drunk that they assumed shooting into an Indian village was not a crime. After due deliberation, the jury, which already had acquitted Plummer, found Mitchell, Reeves, and Moore guilty, their punishment to be banishment from the community. A later poll revealed that one juror—N. P. Langford—had voted for death, the overall count being eleven to one for banishment. From that day on, Langford himself would be marked for death, so far as gang members were concerned.

Because the weather was so cold and the snow so deep in the surrounding mountain passes that travel would be hazardous to their health, the three convicted men were permitted to remain in the area for the time being. Mitchell never did leave Bannack, while Moore and Reeves went only as far as the town of Deer Lodge, a day or two's journey north toward Butte.

To the gang members, the verdict and light sentences proved that they were still running things in this part of the country. Dimsdale writes:

> "During the trial the roughs would swagger into the space allotted for the Judge and jury, giving utterance to clearly understood threats, such as, 'I'd like to see the G-d d----d jury that would dare to hang Charley Reeves or Bill Moore,' etc., etc., which doubtless had fully as much weight with the jury as the evidence had. The pretext of the prisoners that the Indians had killed some whites, friends of theirs, in '49 while going to California was accepted by the majority of the jurors as some sort of justification; but the truth is, they were afraid of their

lives—and it must be confessed, not without apparent reason."

Dimsdale concludes his account of the first public trial in Montana by complaining mournfully:

> "Had the question been left to old Californians or experienced miners, Plummer, Reeves, and Moore would have been hanged, and much bloodshed and suffering would have thereby been prevented. No organization of the road agents would have been possible."

But for Henry Plummer and his friends, the way now seemed clear to operate with impunity and no fear of reprisal. Which they proceeded to do . . .

7

DAYS OF POWER
FOR THE PLUMMER GANG

On three different occasions following his appointment as sheriff, Hank Crawford tendered his resignation, only to have it rejected by his Law and Order friends, who promised to stand by him in the execution of his duties and to reimburse him for his expenditure of time and money.

Instead of paying Crawford in cash, they suggested that he take his expenses and salary out of the money he would receive from the sale of the firearms and horses confiscated from the convicted men, Reeves, Moore, and Mitchell, as well as from Henry Plummer, who had taken over the property of the late Jack Cleveland.

In order to do this, of course, Crawford would have to go and collect the valuables, which should have been no problem. After all, he *was* the sheriff.

At the time of his death, Jack Cleveland owned three horses, one of which was at a ranch near Bannack City, while the other two were pastured on the Big Hole River. In a meeting of the Law and Order people, Sheriff Crawford was authorized to go and get them. But before he could do that, a man named Old Tex, who was a member of the Plummer Gang, called a "miners" meeting of gang members, which decreed that the horses belonged to a man named Terwilliger, who had been

Jack Cleveland's partner. Since Terwilliger was absent for the time being, it would not be right for Sheriff Crawford to take the horses until the title question was settled, now would it? Why not leave the animals where they were until he got back?

Reluctantly, Sheriff Crawford agreed, stipulating that nobody was to ride the horses until the title business was settled.

A few days later, Henry Plummer was seen mounted on one of the animals. When accused of using it without authorization, he said he was merely riding it to escort the men sentenced to be banished, who, because of inclement weather, had gone only as far as Deer Lodge. On this occasion, he did return the horse to the Bannack ranch. But gang members soon were riding it and the other horses, in brazen defiance of the agreement made between Old Tex and Sheriff Crawford.

At the "miners" meeting called by Old Tex, it had also been resolved that the firearms should be returned to the banished men by the sheriff, which he reluctantly did when his Law and Order supporters showed by their silence that they had no objection. This meant that he had no property to reclaim in lieu of a salary.

"Popular institutions are of divine origin," Dimsdale writes sarcastically. "Government by the people *en masse* is the acme of absurdity."

Emboldened by the fact that the community was not supporting their local sheriff very well, Plummer embarked on a campaign of harassment whose ultimate aim was to provoke Crawford into a gunfight. Well aware of the fact that if he killed Crawford when the sheriff was unarmed or not given a chance to draw a gun, he would be quickly hanged, Plummer played a game of goad and pull back, challenge and withdraw, for several days, without managing to maneuver Crawford into a position where Plummer could shoot him with impunity.

Finally, Plummer went one step too far, sending word to Sheriff Crawford that he would be waiting with a loaded double-barreled shotgun in the doorway of a shop across the street from Goodrich's Saloon, ready to shoot him on sight the moment the sheriff came out of the saloon to face him.

Finding this to be an offer he could not refuse, Sheriff

Crawford accepted it—with a slight modification of terms, which he, as the man challenged, felt it his right to do. Knowing Plummer to be faster on the draw and a better pistol shot than he was, Crawford was not about to engage him in a draw-and-shoot gunfight with revolvers. In such a duel, he knew, Plummer would put a couple of bullets in him before his own six-shooter cleared leather. Plummer had chosen a double-barreled shotgun as his weapon and promised to fire on sight. Sheriff Crawford felt he had the right to use a long-barreled weapon, too—a hunting rifle loaned him by a friend named Frank Ray, who assured him the gun made anything under two hundred yards point-blank range.

Stepping out the door of the Goodrich Saloon, Hank Crawford looked for his opponent, found him right where he had said he would be, raised the rifle and fired. Dimsdale's account of the duel is as brief as the gunfight itself:

> "He (Crawford) instantly leveled at Plummer and fired. The ball broke his *(Plummer's)* right arm. His friends gathered around him, and he said, 'Some son of a b----h has shot me.' He was then carried off."

Because it was well known that Plummer had set the terms of the encounter as a "shoot-on-sight" affair and was carrying a loaded-and-cocked double-barreled shotgun when Crawford fired the shot that disabled him, gang members could not claim it had not been a fair fight. Next day, after the town doctor patched him up, Plummer asked for a re-match, challenging Crawford to meet him again in fifteen days. According to Dimsdale:

> "But he (Crawford) paid no attention to a broken-armed man's challenge, fifteen days ahead . . . Some of the citizens, hearing of this, offered to shoot or hang Plummer, if Crawford would go with them; but he refused, and said he would take care of himself . . ."

Hank Crawford decided the best way to take care of himself was to retire from the sheriff business, which he was growing to dislike, and get out of the territory. He left Bannack and returned to his former home in Wisconsin, vowing not to come back to Montana until it became more civilized—if ever it did.

As for Henry Plummer, his wounded right arm never did regain its former suppleness. And practice assiduously though he did at drawing and shooting left-handed, his skill as a southpaw gunfighter remained far below what it had been right-handed . . .

With its sheriff departed and the Law and Order people showing little interest in keeping the roughs in line, the Plummer Gang became bolder in its operations, robbing and killing with little fear of apprehension. Witnesses who had testified against Mitchell, Reeves, and Moore were so relentlessly harried, harassed, and threatened that many of them left Montana Territory and returned to the states. Nathaniel Langford, the only jury member to vote for death rather than banishment, "was an especial object of hatred to them," Dimsdale writes, "and marked for assassination."

But Langford was not a soft target. He and a friend named Sam Hauser had developed a rich placer claim, a sawmill, a general merchandise store, and other businesses so profitable that when they made shipments of gold to Salt Lake City they could hire enough teamsters and guards to make up a train of seven or eight wagons carrying as much as $75,000 in treasure. Just before one such trip, Dimsdale writes, Langford displayed a precaution he was taking against robbery:

> "Hauser had that morning communicated to his friend Langford his suspicion that they were being watched, and would be followed by road agents, with the intention of plundering them. While Langford was loading his gun with twelve revolver balls in each barrel, George Dart asked him why he was 'filling the gun-barrel so full of lead'; to which Langford replied that if they had any trouble with road agents, it would be on that night."

Neither the allegiance of George Dart nor the nature of

the twin-barreled weapon loaded with twelve revolver balls is clarified by Dimsdale. But the message conveyed to potential road agents must have been crystal clear: an attack on the Langford train would be met with considerable resistance.

Still masquerading as a friendly sort of person concerned about his fellow man's health and well-being, Henry Plummer visited Sam Hauser in the wagon yard where the shipment was being assembled the morning of the winter day it was scheduled to leave.

"You'll be doing some cold traveling, Sam," he told Hauser. "I brought you a present you'll find useful on the way."

The present was a distinctive red, yellow, and black woollen scarf, an easily recognizable means, Hauser knew, by which Plummer's holdup men could identify the person in charge. As usual, Henry Plummer himself would leave Bannack several hours before the wagon train departed, riding in a northwesterly direction while the freight wagons traveled southeast, so that he would have an iron-clad alibi when the train was attacked and robbed.

As an excuse for leaving Bannack, Plummer would say he had received an urgent request from a group of prospectors who thought they had found a rich silver vein in a remote spot in the mountains which neither he nor they would reveal. As yet, no deposits of silver had been found in this part of Montana, but where there was gold there was often silver. Having lived in Nevada where great silver bonanzas had been found a few years ago, Henry Plummer was known to be the resident expert on silver. Public-spirited person that he was, he was always willing to share his knowledge with a free appraisal.

That his secretive silver vein appraisal trips often coincided with robberies and murders along the trail in an opposite direction was just that—a coincidence.

By now, Plummer Gang members dominated the "miners" meetings where camp law was made and administered. With a heavy snowpack still blocking the trails, two of the banished men, Charley Reeves and Bill Moore, could get no farther than Deer Lodge, while the third, William Mitchell, never left Bannack. So it was not surprising that the gang members should show great compassion for their not-quite-departed friends. Dimsdale writes:

> "Finding that Mitchell had not gone away from town, a great many citizens thought it would be the height of injustice to keep Moore and Reeves away . . . on Sunday, a miners meeting was called, at which their sentence was remitted, by vote, and they accordingly came back."

So once again, the roughs were in control.

Now that they were back in the saddle, Henry Plummer wasted no time in calling for an election in which his people would be the only candidates. By then, there had been a major distraction when, in early June 1863, the fabled Mother Lode called Alder Gulch had been discovered by Tom Cover, Bill Fairweather, Barney Hughes and "some others" Dimsdale does not name.

> "It was sheer accident. After a long and unsuccessful tour they came thither on their way to Bannack, and one of them took a notion to try a pan of dirt. A good prospect was obtained, and the lucky 'panner' gave his name to the far-famed 'Fairweather District.'"

During the next few years, at least $100 million in treasure would be taken out of Alder Gulch. To most of the gold-crazed men that poured into this remote part of the country, law enforcement was a minor concern. So no one noticed or cared when Henry Plummer got himself elected sheriff of Bannack, despite his known criminal character. His first official act was to appoint two of his gang member friends, Buck Stinson and Ned Ray, as deputies. According to Dimsdale:

> "Nor did he remain contented with that, but he had the effrontery to propose to a brave and good man in Virginia City that he should make way for him there, and as certain death would have been the penalty for a refusal, he consented. Thus Plummer was actually Sheriff of both places at once. This politic move threw

the unfortunate citizens into his hands completely, and by means of his robber deputies—whose legal functions cloaked many a crime—he ruled with a rod of iron."

Also appointed as deputy sheriff was gang member Jack Gallagher, while another deputy named Dillingham, whose subsequent actions made gang members suspect him to be a Law and Order man, was left to serve out his term in the Virginia City district. Overhearing Buck Stinson, Haze Lyons, and Charley Forbes make plans to hold up and rob a Virginia City-bound man named Dodge, Dillingham made the mistake of warning Dodge about their plans. Foolishly, Dodge then confronted the three would-be robbers, whose first reaction was to deny that they had any such plans; their second, a determination to kill Dillingham for his act of disloyalty to gang principles.

Encountering Dillingham on the road, the three men pressed him between them. Dimsdale relates what followed:

"'We want to see you,' said Haze. Stinson walked a pace or two ahead of the others. Haze was on one side and Forbes was behind. 'Bring him along! Make him come!' said Buck Stinson, half turning and looking over his shoulder. They walked on about ten paces, when they all stopped, and the three faced toward Dillingham. 'Damn you, take back those lies!' said Haze, and instantly the three pulled their pistols and fired, so closely together that eyesight was a surer evidence of the number of shots discharged than hearing. There was a difference, however. Haze fired first, his ball taking effect in the thigh. Dillingham put his hand to the spot and groaned. Stinson's bullet went over his head, but Charley Forbes' shot passed through his breast. On receiving the bullet in the chest, Dillingham fell like an empty sack. He was carried into a brush wakiup and lived but a very short time."

Deputy Sheriff Jack Gallagher settled the matter very neatly and effectively for his friends, Dimsdale says, by reloading their pistols so that no one could tell who had fired the fatal shots, if indeed any shots had been fired. But too many people had witnessed the deed to let Deputy Gallagher get away with that, so the three men were seized by a group of citizens, a captain of the guard was elected, and a detail of miners took charge of the prisoners. Shortly thereafter, a people's court was organized and the trial commenced. Dimsdale describes the events:

"It was a trial by the people *en masse*. For our own part, knowing as we do the utter impossibility of all the voters hearing half the testimony, seeing also that the good and bad are mingled, and that a thief's vote will kill the well-considered verdict of the best citizens, in such localities and under such circumstances verdicts are as uncertain as the direction of the wind on next Tibb's Eve. We often hear of the justice of the masses 'in the long run'; but a man may get hung 'in the short run' or may escape the rope he has so remorselessly earned, which is, by a thousand chances to one, the more likely result of a mass trial. The chance of a just verdict being rendered is almost a nullity . . . if they do right, it is by mistake."

Considering the handicaps of poor lighting, chilled fingers, and hand-set type under which a frontier editor labored in those days, Dimsdale cannot be blamed for the fact that his text is sometimes jumbled and disjointed. Even so, a gem-like figure of speech often sparkles in his prose, as when he comments on the vagaries of decisions made *en masse*:

"Such favors are distributed like sailors' prize money, which is nautically supposed to be sifted through a ladder. What goes through is for the officers; what sticks to the rounds is for the men."

In a curious reversal of the earlier trial, when a majority of the miners insisted that a jury of twelve respected solid citizens be selected to sit in judgment, the Law and Order faction this time favored an *en masse* trial. The reason for their change in attitude was simple. According to the law, the jury was selected by the sheriff. With his own people on trial, Sheriff Plummer would make sure the twelve tried-and-true men picked as jurors were gang members.

No courthouse or jail had yet been built. The charred canyon of Alder Gulch, whose growth of trees already had been destroyed by carelessly set campfires, served as the Hall of Justice. The Throne of Judgment containing the accused, the attorneys, and the judge was the box of a wagon parked in the middle of the town's only street. Dimsdale writes:

> "The trial commenced by the indictment of Buck Stinson and Haze Lyons, and continued till dark, when court adjourned. The prisoners were placed under a strong guard at night. They were going to chain them, but they would not submit. Charley Forbes said he 'would suffer death first.' This of course suited the guard of miners, and quick as a flash came down six shotguns in line with Charley's head. The opinion of this gentleman on the subject of practical concatenation underwent an instantaneous change. He said mildly, 'Chain me.'"

Late that night after the other prisoners and most of the camp had gone to sleep, Haze Lyons sent for the captain of the guard, then told him he had a confession to make.

> "I want you to let these men off. I am the man that killed Dillingham. I came over to do it, and these men are innocent. I was sent here by the best men in Bannack to do it."

Upon being asked who the best men in Bannack were, he named several gang members, then added, "Henry Plummer told me to shoot him."

The first half of that statement was an "impossible falsehood," Dimsdale says; the last half "exactly true."

The captain of the guard was not impressed. Next morning after breakfast the trial resumed, concluding at noon. Dimsdale writes:

"The attorneys had by this time finished their pleas, and the question was submitted to the people, 'Guilty or not Guilty?' A nearly unanimous verdict of 'Guilty' was returned. The question as to the punishment was next submitted by the President, and a chorus of voices from all parts of the vast assembly shouted, 'Hang them.' Men were at once appointed to build a scaffold and to dig the graves of the doomed criminals."

Meanwhile, Charley Forbes, whose trial had been separated from that of the other two men for no apparent reason other than the fact he was "a splendid looking fellow straight as a ramrod, handsome, brave, and agile as a cat in his movements," was brought before the court, whose *en masse* jury was getting bored with the whole process.

Dimsdale said many believed Forbes was faster than Plummer at handling his revolver. Forbes "had the scabbard sewn to the belt, and wore the buckle always exactly in front, so that his hand might grasp the butt, with the forefinger on the trigger and the thumb on the cock, with perfect certainty, whenever it was needed, which was pretty often."

Forbes was also a literate man, Dimsdale admits with the grudging admiration of an Oxford-educated editor, saying, "Charley had corresponded with the press, some articles on the state and prospects of the Territory having appeared in the California papers, and were very well written."

If his good looks and literary ability were not enough to secure his acquittal, he had other factors going for him— namely, Jack Gallagher's grabbing and reloading his pistol so that it appeared not to have been fired, despite the fact that a number of witnesses had seen him trigger the fatal shot into Dillingham's breast. The "softness" of the hundreds of men and a dozen or two women in the crowd was deplored by Dimsdale, who wrote:

"Charley was acquitted by a nearly unanimous vote. Judge Smith, bursting into tears, fell on his neck and kissed him, exclaiming, 'My boy! my boy!' Hundreds pressed round him, shaking hands and cheering, till it seemed to strike them all at once that there were two men to hang, which was even more exciting, and the crowd 'broke' for the 'jail.'"

The excitement of the killing, the two-day trial, and the fact that everyone present was taking part in a life-or-death decision must have encouraged the participants—including Judge Smith—to do quite a bit of drinking, for the crowd was getting maudlin. Just who the ladies were is not clarified by Dimsdale, though his comments on the nature of the fair sex as a whole were specific enough. Like all gold-boom towns, Virginia City had attracted a number of prostitutes, a class of women notoriously soft-hearted where handsome men were concerned. Also present were the wives of a few merchants and tradespeople, women usually sheltered from witnessing acts of violence, Dimsdale says.

When a wagon was drawn up and the two condemned men ordered to get in it for their ride to the gallows, several of their drunken friends clambered in with them, vowing to accompany their buddies to the foot of the scaffold, at least. Dimsdale describes the lachrymose scene that followed:

"At this juncture Judge Smith was called for, and then, amidst tremendous excitement and confusion, Haze Lyons crying and imploring mercy, a number of ladies, much affected, begged earnestly to 'Save the poor young boys' lives.' The ladies admit the crying but declare that they wept in the interest of fair play. One of them saw Forbes kill Dillingham, and felt that it was popular murder to hang Stinson and Lyons, and let off the chief desperado because he was good-looking. She had furnished the sheet with which the dead body was covered."

It is here that Thomas Dimsdale expresses his opinion of women in general from which we must distance ourselves with the disclaimer that it is his opinion, not ours, and he alone should be called upon to answer for it. He writes:

"We cannot blame the gentle-hearted creatures; but we deprecate the practice of admitting the ladies to such places. They are out of their path. Such sights are unfit for them to behold, and in rough and masculine business of every kind women should bear no part. It unsexes them, and destroys the most lovely parts of their character. A woman is a queen in her own home; but we neither want her as a blacksmith, a plough woman, a soldier, a lawyer, a doctor, nor in any such professions or handicraft. As sisters, mothers, nurses, friends, sweethearts, and wives, they are the salt of the earth, the sheet anchor of society, and the humanizing and purifying element in humanity. As such, they cannot be too much respected, loved, and protected. From Blue Stockings, Bloomers, and strong-minded she-males generally, 'Good Lord, deliver us.'"

When a gang member friend of Haze Lyons produced a letter of farewell the condemned man supposedly had written his mother, cries went up from the ladies, "Read the letter!" After this was done amid piteous sobs and sighs, another cry arose from the fair sex and his gang member friends, "Give him a horse and let him go to his mother!"

By popular demand, another voice vote was taken as to the guilt or innocence of the two once-convicted men, but the number of shouted "ayes" and "nays" was so evenly balanced that no decision could be made. It was then ordered that the people in favor of hanging move up-hill, while those favoring acquittal go down-hill.

"The down-hill men claimed that the prisoners were acquitted, but the up-hills would not give way. All this time confusion reigned around the wagon."

The third vote was managed in a different way, with two pairs of men being chosen, the idea being that those favoring carrying out the hangings would pass between one pair, while those who favored setting the accused men free would go between the other pair. A not entirely unbiased reporter, Dimsdale claims the freedom advocates cheated, writing:

> "The latter party ingeniously increased their vote by the simple but efficient expedient of passing through several times, and finally an honest Irish miner, who was not so weak-kneed as the rest, shouted out, 'Be ----, there's a bloody booger voted three times!'"

Flushed out of the voting line, Dimsdale says, the triple voter fled into the nearby brush, but his and a number of other gang member ballots had already been counted—a fact now emphasized by Deputy Sheriff Jack Gallagher, who brandished his pistol and shouted:

"Let them go! They're cleared!"

Amid confused, contradictory cries from a thousand throats, the final verdict was sealed when Haze Lyons and Buck Stinson, " . . . seeing a horse with an Indian saddle, belonging to a Blackfoot squaw, seized it, and mounting both on the same animal, rode at a gallop out of the Gulch."

Knowing their cause was lost, the guards did not pursue them. But one of them observed wryly to another as he gestured up at the unused gallows, "There is a monument of disappointed justice."

Meanwhile, the body of the victim of the pardoned killers lay stark and stiff on a gambling table in a brush wakiup nearby. Dimsdale writes:

> "Judge Smith came to X (John X. Beidler), and asked if enough men could be found to bury Dillingham. X said there were plenty, and, obtaining a wagon, they put the body into a coffin, and started toward the graveyard on Cemetery Hill, where the first grave was opened in Virginia City to receive the body of the murdered man."

Dimsdale said as the funeral procession moved up the hill, a local merchant observed proudly to Judge Smith:

"'Only for my dear wife and daughter, the poor fellows would have been hanged.'

"'How kind of them,' another man said sarcastically. 'They had tears a-plenty to shed for the murderers, I notice, but none for poor Dillingham.'

"'Oh,' said the merchant, 'I cried for Dillingham.'

"'Darned well you thought of it,' replied the mountaineer."

By the time the crowd reached the burial grounds it had dwindled to only eight or ten men, one of whom was Judge Smith, who by then was pretty well in his cups, Dimsdale says.

"'Judge, you've been doing a lot of talking for the past three days,'" one of the men said. "'Maybe now you ought to pray.'"

"The individual addressed knelt down and made an appropriate prayer, but it must be stated that he was so intoxicated that kneeling was as much a convenience as it was a necessity. Some men never "experience religion" unless they are drunk . . . The scene closes with the lachrymose or weeping developments, ending in pig-like slumbers. Anyone thus moved by liquor is not reliable."

So once again an openly committed crime witnessed by the entire community and judged by the people *en masse* went unpunished. Small wonder that Henry Plummer and the members of his gang felt that they could do whatever they wanted to do in Alder Gulch and get away with it.

But the time of reckoning was not far away . . .

8

THE INFERNAL TRIANGLE: CHEROKEE BOB, BILL MAYFIELD AND THE LADY KNOWN AS CYNTHIA

The two best sources for the nefarious doings of the Henry Plummer Gang are Thomas Dimsdale and Nathaniel Langford, who were there "when the guns went off," so to speak, and were eye-witnesses to what happened. Both were honest, moral men, whose reliability cannot be questioned. Though they wrote about the same people and the same events, the circumstances under which they set down and published their stories were so different that they must be considered here before their accounts can be compared.

Thomas Dimsdale, an Englishman, was consumptive and in poor health when he came to what soon would be Montana Territory in 1863. A well-educated, non-violent man, he established the first newspaper in the territory, wrote and published a series of articles about the Plummer Gang and the Vigilantes as events occurred, but played no active role in the happenings themselves. Dying in 1866 at the age of thirty-eight, he had no time to pass judgment on the crimes that were committed or the punishments meted out by the peoples' tribunal.

Nathaniel Langford, on the other hand, was in robust health when he came to Bannack in 1863, took an active role in defending his property and his person against members of the Plummer Gang, and did not publish his book *Vigilante*

Days and Ways until 1893. By this time, thirty years later, he and many of the men he wrote about had become substantial citizens of Montana and had acquired both wealth and power. As a member of the executive committee of the Montana Vigilantes, Langford was privy to every decision the committee made. As collector of Internal Revenue for Montana between 1864 and 1868; as a member of the Washburn Yellowstone Expedition in 1870; and as the first superintendent of Yellowstone National Park from its establishment in 1872 until 1877, he wrote a number of articles for national magazines.

But the best indication of the toughness of his character was the fact that during the heyday of the Plummer Gang he never left home without his favorite weapon, a sawed-off shotgun, each of whose twin barrels was loaded with heavy charges of powder and twelve pistol balls. Obviously, he was not a man to be taken lightly.

During the thirty years it took Langford to write and publish his two-volume book, he had ample opportunity to talk to, correspond with, and read the writings of men such as Granville Stuart, William McConnell, and John Hailey. All those men were involved in the Vigilante movements of Montana and Idaho territories and later became governors of those states. Human nature being what it is, these political figures, as well as Nathaniel Langford himself, no doubt put the best interpretation possible on the acts they committed to bring law and order to their part of the world. As for the gang-member side of the story, few if any transgressors survived to write their memoirs.

In any event, when he finally got around to writing and publishing his *Vigilante Days and Ways* in 1893, Nathaniel Pitt Langford related some colorful stories about gang members, not the least of which is the one that follows:

As noted before, during the Civil War period between 1860-65, a second wave of emigration flowed over the Oregon Trail into the Pacific Northwest, impelled by the desire of both Northern and Southern sympathizers to avoid a conflict they did not believe in passionately enough to risk shedding their own blood, though they were not averse to expressing their loyalties in words. When gold and silver strikes were made in Oregon, Montana and Idaho, and, the lure of instant wealth in this lawless land added to the deadly mix of inflamed passions.

Although no treasure ever was found near the southeastern Washington Territory town "they liked so well they named it twice," Walla Walla became a staging area and

Vigilante Days and Ways
Nathaniel P. Langford

outfitting point for the Idaho and Montana mines during the early 1860s, as well as a frontier cavalry post manned by blue-clad Union soldiers. Like many other frontier settlements, the town supported a number of saloons, entertainment parlors, and theaters. These establishments were well patronized by soldiers, gamblers, and roughs whose crimes ranged from petty thefts to brutal murders. The atmosphere in which the plays were staged is vividly described by Langford:

"No person who has witnessed a theatrical performance in a mining camp can forget the general din and noise with which the audience fill up the intervals between the acts. Whistling, singing, hooting, yelling, and a general shuffling of feet and moving about are so invariable as to form, in fact, a feature of the performance. So long as they are unaccompanied by quarrelsome demonstrations and do not become too boisterous, efforts are seldom made to suppress them. The boys are permitted to have a good time in their own way, and the lookers-on, accustomed to the scene, are often compensated for any annoyance that may be occasioned, by strokes of border humor more enjoyable than the play itself."

But the "annoyance" planned by Cherokee Bob Talbert, who became an early recruit in the Henry Plummer Gang, went far beyond the limits of "border humor." What he proposed to do, with the connivance of local Deputy Sheriff Porter, who like himself was a Secessionist, was create a disturbance in the theater during whose confusion he would pick a quarrel with then shoot and kill a number of Federal soldiers.

According to Langford, Cherokee Bob was a native Georgian who received his name from the fact that he was a quarter-blood Indian, with good reason to be bitter about the Union. Maniac in his adherence to the cause of Secession, he could talk or think of little else than the great inferiority of the Northern to the Southern soldiers, and was continually bragging about his own superior physical power. It was his frequent boast that, aided by a Negro servant carrying two baskets filled with loaded pistols, he could "put to flight the bravest regiment of the Federal army."

That he made this statement in the far western town of Walla Walla rather than in a combat zone near Gettysburg or Bull Run was not of course called to his attention by his friends.

On the evening of the incident, six or seven soldiers were seated in the theater, with Deputy Porter, Cherokee Bob, and several of his ruffian friends nearby. When the curtain fell on the first act, the soldiers began making the usual loud, hooting noises. Porter jumped up from his seat and cried,

"Dry up, you brass-mounted hirelings, or I'll snatch you bald-headed!"

"Why do you pick on us?" a soldier demanded, "when there are others more boisterous?"

Waiting for no further provocation, Deputy Porter drew and cocked his revolver, grabbed one of the soldiers by the collar of his blouse, and started dragging him across the floor, at the same time calling for the assistance of Cherokee Bob and his friends. When the soldier offered resistance, a melee developed. Women and children in the audience screamed in fright. The other soldiers present rushed to the rescue of their comrade with drawn pistols.

"Cherokee Bob with a pistol in one hand and a Bowie knife in the other, his voice wildly ringing above all other sounds, was in his true element," Langford writes. "More than a dozen pistol shots followed in quick succession. Two of the soldiers were killed, and others fearfully mangled."

Next day, when the enlisted men appealed to the commanding officer at Fort Walla Walla to take action, his response was to order the soldiers involved placed under arrest, then dismissed the subject from his mind.

But the soldiers weren't ready to let the matter drop. About fifty of the troopers armed themselves, and marched into town, determined to capture and hang Cherokee Bob, whom they knew to be the chief mover behind the assault. Forewarned of their coming, Cherokee Bob stole a horse and left town, heading east to Lewiston, where he went to work as a gambler in a saloon with a former friend and fellow member of the Plummer Gang, Bill Mayfield.

"Here he trumped up an intimacy," Langford writes, "with a woman calling herself Cynthia, at that time stewardess of a hotel in Lewiston, and the fallen wife of a very worthy man."

Giving the reader no more information on the background of the Lady Known as Cynthia, Langford says that the star-crossed trio soon traveled east to the gold-boom town of Florence, where Bill Mayfield began to grow irritated at the attentions of Cherokee Bob to his mistress. As for the lady herself:

"Cynthia possessed many charms of person, and considerable intelligence. She had, moreover, an eye to the main chance, and was ready to bestow her favors where they would command the most money. Bob was richer than Mayfield, and this fact won him many encouraging smiles from the fair object of his pursuit. Mayfield's jealousy flamed into anger, and he resolved to bring matters to a crisis, which should either secure his undisturbed possession of the woman, or transfer her to the sole care of his rival."

Langford then commits the cardinal sin of factual writing when he ascribes thoughts and feelings to actual people with no proof that they really had them:

"Mayfield had confidence enough in Cynthia, to believe when required to choose between him and Cherokee Bob, her good taste, if nothing else, would give him the preference."

This did not prove to be the case. Discussing the problem in her presence like civilized people, both men laid hands on the butts of their holstered revolvers from time to time, saying such things as:

"Bob, you know me,"

and,

"Yes, Bill, and you know me,"

then,

"Well now, Bob, the question is whether we should make fools of ourselves."

The final outcome of their intellectual discussion was that rather than engaging in a shootout in which one or both of them might get hurt, they would settle the question by asking the Lady Known as Cynthia which man she preferred. Like most classic love-triangles, other versions of the story exist, such as: (1) that the two men played a hand of poker, with Cynthia as the stakes, and that Cherokee Bob won her, fair and square; (2) that he won her, but cheated; (3) that Cynthia was so offended by being tossed into the pot that she accepted neither man, running off with a total stranger, who soon deserted her, after which neither of her former lovers wanted her. But since this is Langford's story, we shall let him conclude it his way:

"What say you, Cynthia?" Mayfield inquired. "Is it Bob or me?"

"Well, William," Cynthia replied with Portia-like logic, "Robert is settled in business now. Don't you think he is better able to take care of me than you are?"

For the reader not familiar with Shakespeare, we should explain that Portia was the lady judge in the *Merchant of Venice* who had to decide whether Shylock the Lender could collect his pound of flesh closest to the heart of his defaulting debtor. She ruled that he could, with this caveat: if he took a single drop of blood with the pound of flesh, he would forfeit his own life.

Convinced that his lady love was lost, Mayfield made a graceful surrender to his rival, saying:

"Well, Bob, you fall heir to all the traps and things there are around here."

Which category the Lady Known as Cynthia fell into is not made clear, but she did show that she retained a real affection for her former lover by shedding a few tears over him, then, a year or so later when she heard that he had come to a violent end, swearing that she would kill his murderer, if ever given the opportunity to do so.

An explanation of the circumstances under which Cherokee Bob became "settled in business" is not the least part of the narrative, Langford writes. Shortly after Bob's arrival in Florence, he learned that a saloon owner friend to whom he recently had loaned some money had died. Approaching the man's partner, Bob told him about the debt, then said he was taking over the saloon and all its contents in payment.

"How much did you loan my partner?" the man inquired. "I'll pay off the debt with interest."

"That's not the idea," rejoined Bob. "Do you think me fool enough to lend a fellow five hundred dollars, and then after it increases to five thousand dollars, square the account with a return of what I lent and a little more?"

Whatever the man's thoughts were, he knew better than

to express them aloud, for by then the Henry Plummer Gang controlled the law enforcement business in this part of the country. Just to make sure he understood that fact, Cherokee Bob gave him twenty-four hours to complete an inventory of the property prior to leaving town for good. Langford writes:

> "So when Bob, accompanied by two or three confederates, came the next morning to the saloon to take possession, he (the former partner) was prepared to submit to the imposition without resistance. Walking within the bar, Cherokee Bob emptied the money drawer and gave the contents to his victim. He then invited his friends to drink to the success of the new enterprise."

This was the manner in which he became, as Cynthia said, "settled in business."

Even though he now owned the saloon free and clear and was doing a lively business so far as volume was concerned, there were some drawbacks to the trade. At any given hour, ten or twelve members of the Plummer Gang were hanging around, playing cards, having drinks, and mingling with miners who had struck it rich in order to learn when and by what route they planned to make their next shipment of gold dust out of town. Once obtained, this information would be passed on to affiliates who would attack and kill any one who resisted giving up their treasure. Whether the desperadoes were paid salaries or worked on commission, Langford does not say. But since mining camp saloons stayed open around the clock, "At all hours of the day and night some of them were to be seen in the two saloons kept by Cherokee Bob and his new partner, Bill Willoughby. When one company disappeared another took its place, and at no time were there less than twenty or thirty of these desperadoes at one place or the other."

Quenching the thirst of these men probably was considered part of the cost of doing business, but it must have cut into the net profit.

When snow blocked the trails to the high country, times got very dull in gold-boom towns such as Florence, Cynthia discovered, creating a winter of discontent. So any event promising music, dancing, bright lights, and laughter was looked forward to with great relish. Langford writes:

> "The New Year was approaching. The good wives and daughters, in accordance with usual custom, proposed that it should be celebrated with a ball, a proposition to which the other sex joyfully acceded. Extensive preparations were made for the supper and the ball-room attractively decorated. Cynthia made known to Bob her desire to go. He said in reply, 'You shall go, and be respected like a decent woman ought to be.'"

The assumption must be made that the town of Florence now contained enough wives and daughters of honest tradespeople to make up a class of society that demanded civilized behavior from persons attending its functions. Other than the fact that Bill Willoughby was "a suspected member" of the Plummer Gang nothing is known about his community standing, but it must have been higher than that of Cherokee Bob, who asked him to take Cynthia to the ball.

"If things don't go right," Bob told Willoughby, "just report to me." Langford writes:

> "Cynthia consented to the arrangement, and Willoughby promised compliance. The guests had arrived when Cynthia, hanging on the arm of Willoughby, made her appearance. Scowls and sneers met them on every hand. A general commotion took place among the ladies. In little groups of five or six, scattered throughout the room, they whispered to each other their determination to leave if Cynthia were permitted to remain. The managers held a consultation, and Willoughby was told he must take Cynthia home. No alternative presenting, he obeyed."

Next day, Cherokee Bob marshalled his forces to avenge the insult, only to find as his gun-fighters roamed the town that a surprisingly large number of townspeople were prepared to meet bullet with bullet. The chief leader of the law and order contingent, Bob learned, was the stubborn, muscular, fearless owner of a rival saloon, a man named "Jakey" Williams. According to Langford:

> "He had been the hero of more than one desperate affray, and was regarded by Bob and Willoughby as the only obstacle in the way of their bloody project to kill the managers of the ball. The first act, therefore, in their contemplated tragedy was to dispose of him. Jakey at first sought to avoid them. They pursued him from house to house, till, tired of fleeing, he finally declared he would go no farther."

By now, the fighting up and down the streets of the town had become general, with the number of law and order people seizing arms and joining the fray growing while the ranks of the gang members were thinned by casualties and desertions. Taking a pot-shot at Jakey Williams just as he ducked into the doorway of his saloon, Cherokee Bob was sure he had killed his arch-enemy, so he turned the muzzle of his pistol on other opponents. This gave Jakey, who had not even been wounded, a chance to grab a double-barreled shotgun, with which he blasted away at Willoughby. Bleeding from multiple wounds, Willoughby cried,

"For God's sake, don't shoot me any more. I'm dying now."

Langford says:

> "Bob beat a retreat at the first fire. Dodging behind a corner, where his head only was exposed, he fired upon his pursuers until his pistols were nearly empty. While aiming for another shot, a ball fired from an opposite window brought him to earth, mortally wounded. He was taken to his saloon, and died the third day after the affray."

Though Cherokee Bob Talbert died believing he had killed the man who had led the local movement to disrespect his lady love, all he had done was deprive her of her two principal protectors, himself and Bill Willoughby, thereby exposing her to the slings and arrows of a hostile social world. Seeing no future for herself in Florence, Cynthia fled south to Boise City, where she joined her former lover, Bill Mayfield.

According to Langford:

> "This reunion was destined to be of short duration. The following spring Mayfield went to Placerville, Idaho, for a brief sojourn. A quarrel over a game of cards sprung up between him and one Evans. Mayfield drew his revolver, intending to settle it by a fatal shot, but Evans interspersed:
>
> "'I am not heeled.'
>
> "'Then go and heel yourself,' said Mayfield, sheathing his revolver, "'and look out the next time you meet me, for I am bound to kill you on sight.'"

Thus forewarned, the man named Evans, who appears to have been a greenhorn in the gunfighter game, did indeed go heel himself—in a most sensible way.

Langford says the following day, Mayfield and two friends were walking in the suburbs. They came upon a muddy spot, across which a narrow plank had been laid. They had to cross single file, with Mayfield in the middle. Evans was in a cabin beside the crossing. Grabbing a double-barreled shotgun, he fired through an open window. Mayfield grasped for his revolver, but fell without power to draw it, exclaiming "I'm shot."

Mayfield died within two hours. Langford concludes the story by moralizing with the Scriptural axiom: "With what measure ye mete, it shall be measured to you again."

Put another way, it could be said that, like Ferd Patterson and many other gunfighters, Bill Mayfield went to glory by meeting a man with a faster draw . . .

Because we cannot improve upon Langford's phrasing as he records the eventual fate of the Lady Known as Cynthia, we quote it verbatim here:

> "After Mayfield's death Cynthia entered upon that

career of promiscuous infamy which is the certain destiny of all women of her class. It is written of her that 'she has been the cause of more personal collisions and estrangements than any other woman in the Rocky Mountains.'"

9

JUDGMENT DAY
FOR THE PLUMMER GANG

I t was bitterly ironic, Nathaniel Langford observed, that two unrelated incidents led to the downfall of the Henry Plummer Gang. One was the robbery and murder of a merchant named Lloyd Magruder; the other, the first death from natural causes ever to occur in the Bannack area. The first showed how swiftly justice could be administered, once people decided to act. The second gave law-abiding members of the community an awareness of their power.

In Bannack, crime and violence had gotten so bad, Langford wrote, "that when a murder was committed or a robbery made, people expressed no stronger feelings than that of thankfulness for their own escape."

Langford says a respected citizen named William H. Bell became critically ill with "mountain fever" (probably a form of pneumonia):

> "After his illness had assumed a dangerous form, he made known to myself and others that he was a Mason, and expressed a desire to be buried with Masonic ceremonies . . . A request for all the Masons in the gulch to meet on Yankee Flat was so numerously responded to

that we found it necessary to adjourn to more commodious quarters."

What then occurred in Montana had happened earlier in gold-boom towns all over the West where high-principled men who believed in law and order met as strangers and then learned they were brothers in the Masonic Lodge. According to Langford:

> "The funeral ceremonies, the next day, were conducted by myself. . . How strange it seemed to see this large assemblage, all armed with revolvers and bowie-knives, standing silently, respectfully, around the grave of a stranger, their features now saddened by a momentary thought of the grave and immortality.
>
> "Nor was this all. They learned from what they saw that here was an association bound together by bonds of brotherly love that would stand by and protect all its members in the hour of danger."

Even as the Masons of Bannack were beginning to realize their numbers and power, a heinous crime revealed in a dream to a Lewiston hotelkeeper named Hill Beachey was being unraveled a few hundred miles west.

In August 1863, a Lewiston merchant named Lloyd Magruder left town with sixty laden pack mules, crossed the Bitter Root Mountains to the mining camps of Montana and sold his goods there for $30,000 in gold dust. He headed home in early fall. His party totaled nine men.

As the time came and passed when Magruder should have returned to Lewiston, his hotelkeeper friend, Hill Beachey, grew increasingly worried about his safety. In fact, Beachey had a premonition, a vision, or a dream telling him something terrible had happened. Learning presently that four suspicious-acting men had left some mules and saddles at a ranch near Lewiston, then taken an early stage for Walla Walla, he examined the animals and saddles and recognized them as having belonged to his missing friend. Three of the men in the Magruder party, D. C. Lowry, David Howard, and James Romain, had shady reputations and were reputed to be members of the Plummer Gang, while the fourth, Billy Page, was a witless, spineless fellow. Those four appeared to be the suspicious-acting men who had turned up in Lewiston. It made Beachey positive there had been foul play.

Idaho State Historical Society 2709
Hill Beachy

Hill Beachey's premonition was so strong he went to the acting governor of newly-created Idaho Territory, Secretary William Daniels, and insisted that he be given requisitions on the governors of Oregon, Washington Territory, and California for their assistance in arresting the three suspects. Then he and a man named Tom Pike set out in pursuit of the fugitives. The trail led overland to Walla Walla and Wallula Landing, then downriver by boat to Portland. There, Beachey learned, the four men he wanted had boarded a ship bound for San Francisco.

The nearest point from Portland at which telegraphic communication with San Francisco could be had was Yreka, in northern California. Leaving Tom Pike in Portland to take the next steamer, Beachey rode the stagecoach three days and nights over the worst kind of roads to Yreka, wired a full description of the suspects to the chief of police in San Francisco, and, when the ship made port, they were immediately arrested.

A writ of *habeas corpus* briefly delayed the return of the four men to Lewiston for trial, but the San Francisco court—apparently caring no more for legal nit-picking than Idaho did—denied the writ. On December 7, 1863, the same day the first Legislature convened in Lewiston, Hill Beachey and Tom Pike arrived home with their prisoners.

There were a couple of legal problems to be ironed out. In the first place, there were no bodies to prove that murder had been done. This was neatly solved by a confession from Billy Page relating in horrible detail how Magruder and four other men had been slain and their bodies dumped into a canyon deep in the mountains, where they now lay buried under many feet of snow.

Secondly, Idaho Territory had no Code of Laws. This the Legislature remedied by enacting a Civil and Criminal Code patterned roughly after the Common Law of England. It took effect January 4, 1864. District Court convened in Lewiston January 5, Judge Samuel C. Parks presiding. Howard, Lowry, and Romain were duly tried and convicted. On January 25, Judge Parks sentenced them to be hanged; and on March 4 the sentence was carried out.

Billy Page, who had turned state's evidence, was permitted to depart. The rumor soon floated back that he had been killed—in what manner or by whom no one knew or cared.

Upon the recommendation of Judge Parks, the Legislature passed an appropriation of $6,244 to reimburse Hill Beachey for expenses incurred in the pursuit and capture of the murderers of his friend. When spring at last melted the snows in the high country of the Lolo Trail to the east, Beachey and a party of men journeyed to the canyon into which Billy Page had said the five bodies had been dumped, found the remains exactly where he had said they would be, and gave them a decent burial.

This was early-day Idaho justice—direct, effective, and not subject to appeal. The procedure was noted in Montana . . .

After the funeral of William H. Bell, members of the Masonic order living in the Bannack area met frequently to discuss matters of mutual interest. Fearful that they were discussing him and his gang members, which they were, Henry Plummer tried to infiltrate the meetings so that he could find out what was going on. When that effort failed, he attempted to ingratiate himself with men who were Masons so that they would endorse his application for membership in the order. In this, he nearly succeeded.

Despite his charm and persuasive powers, Henry Plummer never managed to become a Mason; nor did any member ever reveal the fact that as much time was being spent in meetings discussing law and order matters as was taken up organizing a lodge chapter in Montana. Indicative of the fear and respect held by the Henry Plummer Gang for Masons was that of the 102 persons murdered by Henry Plummer's gang, not one was a Mason.

Originally part of Idaho Territory, created March 3, 1863, Montana Territory was established a year later, on May 26, 1864. Following the first strike in Bannack in 1862, the Alder Gulch discovery was made in early June 1863. A careless campfire spread by the hot, dry summer wind turned the thick groves of trees in the area to charred ashes in a single night. For a distance of twelve miles along the floor of the gulch, every square foot of gravel soon was claimed, making the region the richest gold-bearing area on earth It eventually became known as Virginia City.

In August 1863, D. S. Payne, the United States Marshal of Idaho, came to Bannack and told Langford he would appoint any person Langford wanted to name as deputy marshal of the Bannack District. As president of the local Union League, most of whose members supported Henry Plummer, Langford told his partner and close friend, Samuel T. Hauser, that he did not intend to vote for Plummer, despite the favorable opinion of most League members. To his surprise, Hauser agreed with him, saying, "Whoever lives to see the gang of highwaymen now infesting the country broken up, will find that Henry Plummer is at the head of it."

With Hauser's support, Langford rejected the advice of the League and opposed Plummer's appointment to the office, which caused U.S. Marshal Payne to refrain from appointing a deputy marshal for the district. Hearing about the rejection, Plummer blustered: "Langford, you'll be sorry for this before the matter ends. I've always been your friend, but from this time on, I'm your enemy; and when I say this, I mean it in more ways than one."

From that day on, Langford went armed at all times, telling only a few trusted friends which horse he would ride and which route he would take between Bannack and Virginia City. At the same time, he made it crystal clear to Henry Plummer that he would not engage in a duel on Plummer's terms, for he knew he could not win a draw-and-shoot gunfight. Instead, he would carry and use his sawed-off, double-barreled, heavily-loaded shotgun, firing at point-blank range the instant he felt himself in danger. This was a weapon that few single-action pistol fighters cared to face.

Later, Langford was told by friends that Henry Plummer tried several times to ambush him when traveling or attempted to take pot-shots at him through the window of his cabin. He was deterred each time by Langford's precautions and the sure knowledge of what would happen if he missed his first shot.

Though deprived of a federal law officer, the miners, merchants, and townspeople in the Bannack-Virginia City area did manage to drum up enough support to elect Henry Plummer sheriff of the district during the summer of 1863, following which most of the deputies he appointed were members of his gang. Before long, he and his henchmen became such a threat to the safety of gold shipments out of the region that only a rare individual made the venture without sending a large escort of well-armed men along as guards.

One of these individuals was Langford's partner, Samuel Hauser, who found a unique way to protect the gold dust he was carrying in a buckskin sack on the stagecoach between Virginia City and Bannack.

Hauser was somewhat surprised on entering the coach at Virginia City to find that he had Plummer for a fellow passenger. Believing that Plummer was going to Bannack to plan means of robbing him, he resolved to act as if he had the most implicit confidence in his integrity. The trip was made in safety, though Hauser confessed that while passing through Rattlesnake Canyon, he did not forget the unenviable notoriety which frequent robberies had gained for it.

When the coach drove up to Goodrich's hotel in Bannack, he felt greatly relieved. In the presence of Judge Edgerton and several other leading citizens, he turned to Plummer, who was standing near, and carelessly addressed him:

"Plummer, I hear that any man who has money isn't safe in this town overnight. I've got fourteen thousand dollars in this bag, which I'm going to take to the States with me when I go. I want you, as sheriff, to keep it for me till I start."

Accepting the gold, Plummer promised to take good care of it and did.

By early January 1864, crime and violence had become so commonplace, Dimsdale wrote, that:

> "Wounded men lay almost unnoticed about the city, and a night or a day without shooting, knifing, or fighting would have been recognized as a small and welcome installment of the millennium. Men dared not go from Virginia to Nevada or Summit after dark. A few out of the hundreds of instances must suffice. A Dutchman, known as Dutch Fred, was met by one of the band, who ordered him to throw up his hands as usual. Finding he had $5 in Treasury notes with him, the robber told him he would take them at par, and added with a volley of curses, 'If ever you come this way again with only $5, I'll shoot you.'"

On second thought, the robber decided to shoot Dutch Fred anyway, wounding him in the arm as a warning to carry more money next time.

Because of the Magruder murders, the current crime conditions, and the knowledge of their power as Masons, the general population needed only a blatant murder or two to stir the Vigilante movement into action. The motivating force came in the form of the cold-blooded killing by George Ives—first of a nameless drifter, then of a well-liked local man named Nicholas Tbalt.

Described as having a rather prepossessing appearance, blue eyes, and light-colored hair, George Ives was clean-shaven and about twenty-seven years old. Dimsdale wrote:

> "Long practice in confronting danger had made him

absolutely fearless . . . He would levy blackmail under the guise of a loan. As a matter of sport, and to show the training of his horse, he would back the animal into the windows of a store, and then ride away laughing."

Hearing that a petty thief had been caught and whipped for stealing, then had tried to ameliorate his punishment by identifying members of the gang for the law and order people, George Ives attacked the luckless man on the road between Bannack and Virginia City. Finding that the buckshot with which his shotgun was loaded did not penetrate the man's buffalo hide coat, Ives then drew his revolver, placed it against the man's head, and coolly shot him dead.

As the murdered man fell from his horse, Ives took the animal by the bridle and led it away. Going to gang member George Hilderman, Ives told him that he would like to stay at his place for a few days, "as he had killed a man near the Cold Spring Ranch, and there might be some stir and excitement about it."

A day or two later, a trader named Nicholas Tbalt sold a span of mules to the firm of Butchey and Clark, who paid him in gold. Taking the dust with him, Tbalt went to Dempsey's Ranch to fetch the animals. When he failed to return, it first was assumed that he had absconded with the money. Then it was learned he had been shot and killed by George Ives, who had ridden up to the shack of a fellow gang member shortly thereafter with both the mules and the gold dust, casually telling his friend that the trader "will never trouble anybody again."

Ten days after the murder, Dimsdale wrote:

"Tbalt's body was finally found where it lay stiff and stark in a sagebrush thicket, whither it had been dragged, unseen of man, but the eye of Omniscience rested on the blood-stained corpse, and the Fiat of the Eternal Judge ordered the wild bird of the mountains (a grouse flew up and revealed its presence) to point out the spot, and, by a miracle, to reveal the crime.

"It was the finger of God that indicated the scene of

the assassination, and it was His will stirring in the hearts of the honest and indignant gazers on the ghastly remains of Tbalt that organized the party which, though not then formally enrolled as a Vigilance Committee, was the nucleus and embryo of the order—the germ from which sprang that goodly tree, under the shadow of whose wide-spreading branches the citizens of Montana can lie down and sleep in peace."

Phrased in less flowery terms, what Dimsdale says is that the orderly society in which Montana residents have lived since that time owes a substantial debt to the boldness with which the Vigilante Committee took the law into its own hands four months before the Territory was organized. The Vigilantes did what they had to do to survive, then passed on an orderly world to their descendants.

After being brought to the Alder Gulch town of Nevada, a few miles west of Virginia City, the body of Nicholas Tbalt lay exposed in the back of a wagon for half a day before a coffin could be found and arrangements made for a decent burial. Dimsdale wrote:

"The indignation of the people was excited by the spectacle. The same afternoon three or four of the citizens raised twenty-five men and left Nevada at 10 p.m. The party subscribed to an obligation before starting, binding them to mutual support, etc., and then travelled on, with silence and speed, towards the valley of the Stinkingwater. Calling at a ranch on their way, they obtained an accession to their numbers, in the person of the man who eventually brought Ives to bay."

At half-past three in the morning the party crossed Wisconsin Creek, seven miles below Dempsey's Ranch, finding it frozen over to the point that the ice in places would carry a man's weight, but not that of a horse. By the time the men dismounted and led their plunging animals across the frigid stream, their clothing was caked with ice, with no fires possible to thaw them out because of the need for secrecy. Calling a halt a mile further on, the leader said,

"Everyone light from his horse, hold him by the bridle, and make no noise till daybreak."

Surrounding a "wakiup" (shack) in front of which several blanket-wrapped figures could be seen reclining on the ground in the gray light of dawn, the leader of the group jumped off his horse and cried,

"The first man that raises will get a quart of buckshot in him, before he can say Jack Robinson."

None of the sleep-befuddled men "raised" or made any sudden moves. The first gang member seized was called "Long John"; he admitted he knew Tbalt had been killed near this very spot and knew George Ives to be the murderer. He had not reported either fact to the authorities, he said, because he feared Ives would kill him. When asked where Ives was now, Long John said he was, "In the wakiup yonder. Give me a minute to put on my moccasins, then I'll take you to him. But I want you to know I did not kill Tbalt. George Ives did."

When the party confronted Ives, he surrendered without resistance, agreeing to go with his captors to Virginia City, where he apparently expected Sheriff Henry Plummer to come to his aid. Also arrested was a gang member identified only as "Tex," who supplied a moment of comic relief when he insisted on taking off his lice-infested shirt and tossing it to one of his captors, saying, "There's my old shirt and plenty of graybacks. You'd better arrest them too."

Writing his account shortly after the arrests had been made and the trials held, Dimsdale is wary about listing names of the Vigilante members. But Langford, who was an active participant in the administration of justice, did not publish his account until thirty years later, so could be very frank in telling the reader who did what to whom. He wrote:

> "Alarmed for the fate of their comrades, the roughs dispatched Clubfoot George (Lane) to Bannack with a message to Plummer, requesting him to come at once to Nevada, and demand the prisoners for trial by the authorities. By means of frequent relays provided at the

several places of rendezvous of the robbers on the route, he performed the ride before morning. Johnny Gibbons, a rancher in sympathy with Ives, proceeded immediately to Virginia City, and secured the legal assistance of Ritchie and Smith, the latter being the same individual who had figured in the defence of the Dillingham murderers."

News of the capture and impending trial of the gang members spread along Alder Gulch as rapidly as the fire that had destroyed the trees the previous summer. By ten o'clock, a crowd estimated at 1,500 to 2,000 men filled the gulch as miners and townspeople poured in. The weather was pleasant for mid-January, with no snow and only a fringe of ice along the banks of the streams. As usual, the first question to be decided was whether the trial should be *en masse* or by a jury selected by Sheriff Henry Plummer. According to Langford:

"It was finally determined that the investigation should be made in the presence of the entire assemblage—the miners reserving the final decision of all questions. To avoid all injustice to people or prisoners, an advisory commission of twelve men from each of the districts was appointed; W. H. Patton of Nevada, and W. Y. Pemberton of Virginia City, were selected to take notes of the testimony."

Appearing as attorneys for the prosecution were Wilbur F. Sanders and Charles S. Bagg, while Alexander Davis and J. M. Thurmond represented the accused. George Ives was the first person put on trial.

Though Dimsdale writes that Henry Plummer responded to news of the impending trial by riding all night on a relay of horses from Bannack to Virginia City, he was conspicuously absent when the trial began the afternoon of January 19, 1864. Nor was he there as it continued for the next two days. The case was given to the jury as night fell January 21. Langford says:

"In less than half an hour they came in with solemn faces with their verdict—Guilty!

"'Thank God for that! A righteous verdict!' and other like expressions broke from the crowd, while on the outer edge of it, amidst mingled curses, execrations, and howls of indignation, and the click of guns and revolvers, one of the ruffians exclaimed,

"'The murderous, strangling villains dare not hang him, at any rate.'"

Instead of asking the twelve-man jury to make this decision, a motion was put to the general assemblage that the report be received, and the jury discharged. Over the objections of the prisoner's lawyers, the motion was carried. Prosecutor Wilbur Sanders then moved, "That George Ives be forthwith hanged by the neck, until he be dead." According to Langford:

"This motion so paralyzed the ruffians, that before they could recover from their astonishment at its being offered, it was carried with even greater unanimity than either of the previous motions, the people having increased in courage as the work progressed . . . Meantime, Ives himself, beginning to realize the near approach of death, begged piteously for a delay until morning, making all those pathetic appeals which on such occasions are hard to resist. 'I want to write to my mother and sister,' said he.

"'Ask him,' said one of the crowd, 'how long a time he gave Tbalt.'"

While he made a will leaving all his earthly goods " . . . to his counsel and companions in iniquity, to the entire exclusion of his mother and sisters," a scaffold was prepared. The butt of a small pine, forty feet in length, was placed inside a half-enclosed building in Virginia City, the top projecting over the cross-beam in front. Near the upper end was fastened the fatal cord, and a large dry-goods box about five feet high was placed beneath for the trap. According to Langford:

"When all the formalities and last requests were over, the order was given to the guards, 'Men, do your duty.'

"The click of a hundred gun-locks was heard, as the guards levelled their weapons upon the crowd, and the box flew out from under the murderer's feet, as he swung in the night breeze, facing the pale moon that lighted up the scene of retributive justice."

Meanwhile, all the gang members in the area were wondering why their chief, Henry Plummer, had not shown up. As sheriff of the district, the least he could do was demand custody of George Ives before he could be tried. If that request were refused, he then should try to obtain a writ of *habeas corpus* in the name of the Territory. But he had not been seen or heard from for several days. Langford also was puzzled by Plummer's absence, writing:

"A saloon keeper by the name of Clinton was very positive that he saw him drink at his bar a few moments before the execution, and that he immediately went out to lead the "forlorn hope" of the roughs. Some other person was probably mistaken for the robber chief, as he was not recognized by any others of the crowd present at the time. In fact, he had enough to do to make provision for his own safety."

Indeed, his own safety must have been his primary concern, for he knew gang member "Red" Yager had given the Vigilante Committee a complete list of the names of men who belonged to the organization, plus their password, their vows, their secret signs, and the special way they knotted their ties so that they might recognize one another on sight. Langford recorded the list for posterity:

"Henry Plummer was chief of the band; Bill Bunton, stool pigeon and second in command; George Brown, secretary; Sam Bunton, roadster; Cyrus Skinner, fence, spy, and roadster; George Shear, horse thief and roadster; Frank Parrish, horse thief and roadster; Haze Lyons, telegraph man and roadster; Bill Hunter, telegraph man and roadster; Ned Ray, council-room keeper at Bannack City; George Ives, Steve Marshland, Dutch John (Wagner), Alex Carter, Whiskey Bill (Graves), Johnny

Cooper, Buck Stinson, Mexican Frank, Bob Zachary, Boone Helm, Clubfoot George (Lane), Billy Terwilliger, Gad Moore, were roadsters.

"These men were bound by an oath to be true to each other, and were required to perform such services as came within the defined meaning of their separate positions in the band. The penalty of disobedience was death. If any of them, under any circumstances, divulged any of the secrets or guilty purposes of the band, he was to be followed and shot down on sight. The same doom was prescribed for any outsiders who attempted an exposure of their criminal designs, or arrested any of them for the commission of a crime. Their great object was declared to be plunder, in all cases without taking life if possible; but if murder was necessary, it was to be committed. Their password was 'Innocent.' Their neckties were fastened with a sailor's knot, and they wore mustaches and chin whiskers. He (Red Yager) was himself a member of the band, but not a murderer."

Organizing the Vigilantes was accomplished as quietly as possible, according to Langford. When completed, it had enrolled "nearly every good citizen in Alder Gulch." Every man whose name appeared on Yager's list was marked for an early examination, and, if found guilty, was to be punished without trial.

"The crisis demanded speedy action . . . It was of special importance that Plummer, the chief of the robber band, should be the first to suffer. The people had found him out, and he knew it."

Reaching Bannack late at night, four Vigilante leaders asked the cooperation of the local citizens in arresting and executing Plummer, Stinson, and Ray. Stinson and Ray were taken without resistance. Then the party detailed to arrest Plummer went to his cabin, where they found him in the act of washing his face. When informed that he was wanted, he appeared to be unconcerned. Quietly picking up a towel to wipe

Montana Historical Society
Henry Plummer was hanged on the gallows he built while sheriff.

his face and hands, he told the leader of the Vigilantes, "I'll be with you in a moment, ready to go wherever you wish. Just let me put on my coat."

Noticing the muzzle of a pistol projecting from under the garment toward which Plummer was moving, one of the party members stepped forward and said helpfully, "I'll hand your coat to you."

Plummer turned deathly pale, for he realized that his last desperate chance to fight for his freedom was gone. Langford writes:

> "With his expertness in the use of that weapon, he would doubtless have slain some or all of his captors. He was marched to a point where he joined Stinson and Ray, and thence the three of them were conducted under formidable escort to the gallows. This structure, roughly framed of the trunks of three small pines, stood in a dismal spot three hundred yards from the centre of the

town. It was erected the previous season by Plummer, who as sheriff had hanged thereon one John Horan, who had been convicted of the murder of Keeley. Terrible must have been its appearance as it loomed up in the bright starlight, the only object visible to the gaze of the guilty men, on that long waste of ghastly snow."

While Ray and Stinson filled the air with curses against the Vigilantes, Henry Plummer politely pleaded for his life. When told the decision to hang him could not be changed, he begged:

"Do with me anything else you please. Cut off my ears, and cut out my tongue, and strip me naked this freezing night, and let me go. I beg you to spare my life. I want to live for my wife—my poor, absent wife. I wish to see my sister-in-law. I want time to settle my business affairs. Oh, God! . . . I am too wicked to die. I cannot go bloodstained and unforgiven into the presence of the Eternal. Only spare me, and I will leave the country forever."

The outlaw leader's pleadings fell on deaf ears.

Kicking, screaming, and cursing to the end, first Ned Ray and then Buck Stinson were hanged. Now that his turn had come, Henry Plummer composed himself, making one final request to the Vigilante who approached him with the rope,
"Give a man time to pray."
"Certainly," replied the Vigilante, pointing up to the cross-beam of the gallows-frame, "but say your prayers up there."
According to Langford:

"The guilty man uttered no more prayers. Standing erect under the gallows, he took off his necktie, and, throwing it over his shoulder to a young man who had boarded with him, he said, 'Keep that to remember me by.' Turning to the Vigilantes, he said, 'Now, men, as a last favor, let me beg that you will give me a good drop.'

"The fatal noose being adjusted, several of the strongest of the Vigilantes lifted the frame of the unhappy criminal as high as they could reach, when, letting it suddenly fall, he died quickly and without a struggle."

At long last, Judgment Day had come for Henry Plummer.

10

AFTERMATH—CLEANING UP THE HUMAN DEBRIS

Arrested with George Ives and brought to Virginia City for trial were two members of the Plummer Gang who supplied a bit of humor to a grim situation. George Hilderman and the man known as "Tex." Tex had insisted that the lice inhabiting his shirt be arrested with him, which was good for a chuckle or two. But George Hilderman had a much greater claim to fame in that he was the model for an episode of gluttony which made the rounds of mining camps in the West for years to come. Physically, George Hilderman was to be pitied, Langford writes, for " . . . he was an old man, weak, somewhat imbecile. . ."

"He was possessed of a coarse humor, which he had lost no opportunity to demonstrate, while a sojourner at Bannack. It made him quite a favorite with the miners, until they became suspicious of his villainous propensities. He was also a notorious 'bummer,' and was oftener indebted to his humor, which was always at command, than his pocket, which was generally empty, for something to eat.

"In width, his mouth was a deformity, and the double row of huge teeth firmly set in his strong jaws gave to his countenance an animal expression truly repulsive. He was the original of the story of 'The Great American Pie-biter.' This feat of spreading his jaws so as to bite through seven of Kustar's dried-apple pies, had been frequently performed by him, in satisfaction of the wager he was ever on hand to make of his ability to do it. On one occasion, however, he was destined to be defeated.

"A miner, who had been victimized by him, arranged with Kustar, the proprietor of the Bannack Bakery, to have two of the pies inserted in the pile without removing the tin plates in which they had been baked, the edges of which were concealed by the overlapping crusts. Hilderman approached the pile, and spreading his enormous mouth, soon spanned it with his teeth. The crunch which followed, arrested by the metal, was unsuccessful. He could not understand it, but, despite the vice-like pressure, the jaws would not close. The trick not being discovered, he paid the wager, declaring that Kustar made the toughest pie-crust he had ever met with."

Even though it became clear during the trial of George Ives that both Tex and George Hilderman knew of the murder of Tbalt and the unknown stranger, when they said that fear of Ives had made them afraid to talk, their pleas were accepted as an amelioration of their crimes. Sentenced to banishment instead of death, they were given ten days to leave the territory, and wisely did so.

Other Plummer Gang members would not be as lucky . . .

Alder Gulch had been the stronghold for the roughs ever since its discovery, Langford writes:

"Being much the largest, richest, and most populous mining camp in the Territory, the opportunities it afforded for robbery were more frequent and promising, and less liable to discovery, than either Bannack or Deer Lodge

. . .

"The Vigilantes, after it was decided to execute

Plummer, comprehended the necessity for prompt and vigorous measures . . . Having ascertained that six of the robber band were still remaining in Virginia City, the Executive Committee decided upon effectual means for their immediate arrest. On the tenth day of January, three days after Plummer was executed, an order was quietly made for the Vigilantes to assemble at night in sufficient force to surround the city. Bill Hunter, one of the six marked for capture, suspecting the plot, effected his escape by crawling beyond the pickets in a drain ditch. The city was encircled, after nightfall, so quietly that none within, except the Vigilantes, knew of it until the next morning."

One man—Jack Gallagher—did have an uneasy feeling that something ominous was going on. While playing faro with a group of friends in a Virginia City saloon, he suddenly threw down his cards and exclaimed,

"While we are here betting, those Vigilantes are passing sentence of death upon us."

How right he was would soon be revealed.

Though Bill Hunter had escaped, five gang members were known to still be in the city: Boone Helm, Jack Gallagher, Frank Parrish, Haze Lyons, and George Lane. With the dawning of a cold, cloudy day, groups of Vigilantes summoned from the adjoining settlements of Nevada, Junction, Summit, Pine Grove, and Highland marched into town in detachments, forming a growing body of men on Main Street. When arrested in a store, the first of the wanted men, Frank Parrish, asked plaintively,

"What am I arrested for?"

"For being a road-agent, thief, and accessory to numerous robberies and murders on the highway."

"I am innocent of all—as innocent as you are."

When confronted with the evidence against him, Parrish changed his story, admitting first to horse stealing, then to butchering stolen cattle for food, to stagecoach robbery, and finally to being a full-fledged member of a gang dealing in plunder and murder.

When Parrish admitted his guilt, he was sentenced to death.

Next to be taken into custody was "Clubfoot" George Lane, who claimed, he was innocent. His accusers said they had positive proof of Lane's guilt and he also received a death sentence.

While George Lane was being questioned, other Vigilantes arrived with Boone Helm and Jack Gallagher. Helm was arrested while standing in front of the Virginia Hotel. He appeared before the judges with an armed man on either side, and one behind with a pistol pointed at his head.

"Ah!" Helm exclaimed, "if I'd only had a show, if I'd known what you were after, you'd have had a gay old time in taking me."

Wounded by a recent accident, Boone Helm had his right hand in a sling and kept fussing with a crude, dirty bandage covering his fingers. Like the others, he swore he was innocent of any crime—a fact to which he was willing to swear on a Bible, should one happen to be handy. According to Langford:

> "Less for any more important purpose than that of testing the utter depravity of the wretch, the interrogator handed him a Bible. With the utmost solemnity of manner and expression, he repeated the denial, invoking the most terrible penalties upon his soul, in attestation of his truthfulness, and kissed the volume impressively at its close."

The interrogator was more horrified and disgusted than impressed. Refusing the offer of a clergyman to help prepare him for his fate, Boone Helm confessed to a murder back in Missouri and another in California before joining the Plummer Gang. When asked to tell what he knew about the band and its crimes, he shrugged and said, "Ask Jack Gallagher. He knows more than I do."

Overhearing the question and reply, Gallagher, who had been brought into an adjoining room separated only by a thin partition, cried out:

> "It is just such cowardly rascals and traitors as you

that have brought us into this difficulty. You ought to die for your treachery."

"I have dared death in all its forms," Helm said indifferently. "I do not fear to die. Give me some whiskey."

"The guilty wretch, having been consigned to the custody of keepers," (Langford writes) "steeped what little sensibility he possessed in whiskey, and passed the time until the execution in ribald jesting and profanity."

When Jack Gallagher was arrested, he bounded into the committee room swearing and laughing, as if the whole affair was intended as a joke, asking, "What is this all about?" On being informed of the charges against him and the sentence of the Committee, he dropped into a chair and began to cry.

Haze Lyons, the only missing gang member being sought, finally was found eating breakfast in a cabin near Virginia City. Caught in the act of raising a piece of griddle cake to his mouth, he surrendered meekly, though he complained the Vigilantes had disturbed the first meal for which he had "any appetite in six weeks."

Lyons was told he could finish his meal but said he was no longer hungry. According to Langford:

"The examination being over, preparations were made for the execution of the convicts. These were very simple. The central cross-beam of an unfinished log store, cornering upon two of the principal streets, was selected for a scaffold. The building was roofless, and its spacious open front exposed the interior to the full view of the crowd. The ropes, five in number, were drawn across the beam to a proper length, and fastened firmly to the logs in the rear basement. Under each noose was placed a large, empty dry-goods box, with cord attached, for the drops."

In addition to the large body of armed Vigilantes, a great number of spectators had assembled from all parts of the gulch, the crowd of 6,000-8,000 people comprising most of the territory's population.

After the prisoners had declined making any final statements, the guards approached to pinion their arms. Swearing, Jack Gallagher, pulled away, drew his pocket-knife, and applied its blade to his throat.

"I will not be hung in public!" he cried. "I will cut my throat first!"

The executive officer pointed his pistol at Gallagher and told the condemned man he would be shot "like a dog," unless he surrendered the knife.

"Don't make a fool of yourself, Jack," advised Boone Helm. "There's no sense in being afraid to die."

Langford said the armed Vigilantes formed around the prisoners, enclosing them in a hollow square. The condemned men were slowly and solemnly marched toward the scaffold.

Spotting a man in the crowd he considered a friend, Clubfoot George Lane called to him, "Judge Dance, we have had dealings together. Can't you say a good word for me?"

When the Judge replied that the evidence against the condemned man was too strong, Lane implored, "Well, then, will you pray with me?"

"Willingly, George; most willingly."

Langford noted that as Clubfoot George, Jack Gallagher, and Judge Dance dropped to their knees and began to pray, Boone Helm, irritated by the delay, raised his sore finger and complained, "For God's sake, if you're going to hang me, do it. If not, I want you to bandage my finger."

While the three men were praying, Haze Lyons begged for permission to see his mistress. He said he wanted to say goodbye and give her back her watch. Remembering what had happened before, the president of the Vigilantes refused the request, saying, "Bringing women to the place of execution 'played out' in '63, Haze, when they interfered with your trial for killing Dillingham."

Conducted into the building, the prisoners were arranged side-by-side. Clubfoot George was first on the east side of the building; next to him was Haze Lyons, then Jack Gallagher, then Boone Helm, and near the west wall Frank Parrish.

After the nooses were adjusted, the chief of the Committee asked the prisoners if they had any last words. Jack Gallagher said he wanted one more drink of whiskey. A nearly full

Montana Historical Society
Virginia City store where Helm, Gallanger, Parrish, Lyons and Clubfoot George were hanged.

tumbler was brought to him and he downed it, though the noose around his neck had to be eased off to give him enough slack to tilt back his head and swallow.

As the guard re-fastened it, Gallagher cried, "I hope Almighty God will curse every one of you, and that I shall meet you all in the lowest pit of hell!"

"No more requests being made. The men laid hold of the cords attached to the box occupied by George Lane. Just at that moment the unhappy wretch descried an old friend clinging to the logs of the building, to obtain sight of the execution.

"'Goodbye, old fellow,' said he. 'I'm gone,' and, without waiting for the box to be removed, he leaped from it, and died with hardly a struggle.

"'There goes one to hell,' muttered Boone Helm.

"Haze Lyons, who stood next, was talking all the

while, telling of his kind mother; that he had been well brought up, but evil associations had brought him to the scaffold.

"Gallagher cried and swore by turns.

"'I hope,' said he, 'that forked lightning will strike every strangling villain of you.' The box, flying from under his foot, stopped the oath in its utterance, and the quivering of his muscles showed that his guilty career was terminated.

"'Kick away, old fellow,' said Boone Helm, calmly surveying the struggles of the dying wretch. 'My turn comes next. I'll be in hell with you in a minute.' Shouting in loud voice, 'Every man for his principles! Hurrah for Jeff Davis! Let her rip,' his body fell with a twang that killed him almost instantly."

Langford says Frank Parrish requested his black necktie be dropped like a veil over his face before he was given the drop. Haze Lyons, after his incessant pleas for mercy were ignored, quieted down and asked that his mistress be given her watch and the disposition of his body. Both men then died without a struggle.

One of the leaders of the Vigilantes, X. Beidler, who was an expert at such matters, had made sure that the nooses were properly adjusted before the drops were made. Earlier, Jack Gallagher had killed one of Beidler's friends. A bystander asked,

"When you came to hang that poor fellow, didn't you sympathize with him, didn't you feel for him"

Langford said Beidler regarded the man for a moment with great disgust and, imitating his tone, replied slowly,

"Yes, I did. I felt for him a little. I felt for his left ear."

Two hours after the execution the bodies were cut down, and taken by friends to Cemetery Hill for burial.

11

MURDER IN HELLS CANYON: THE CHINESE MASSACRE

Thirty-three miles downstream from Lewiston, Idaho, the last dam to be built on the Snake River was completed in 1974. It is called Lower Granite—for no better reason than that it was placed four miles downstream from its original planned site, Granite Point.

By any name, it serves as a tombstone for an obscure alien who, like many of his countrymen, came from South China to *Gum Shan*—the "Golden Hills"—of America during the 1880s to seek his fortune. Instead, he met violent death.

His name was Chea-Yow.

According to a report long buried in State Department files, his body was found on Log Cabin Bar, the exact site of Lower Granite Dam, June 23, 1887, by United States Commissioner J. K. Vincent, who reported it to be:

> ". . . about 5 feet 7 or 8 inches tall; had on clothes and boots; two shot wounds in small of back near backbone; head off, as though chopped; left arm off between elbow and shoulder, both arm and head in coat which was fastened to his body, held there by a belt around his waist. He was lodged in a huge drift pile . . ."

Since Vincent made no effort to remove the corpse so that the bones could be returned to China for proper internment, we must assume this lonely canyon dam site to be the final resting place for Chea-Yow's spirit.

Should it be called Chea-Yow Dam, then, rather than Lower Granite?

Historically, there are precedents enough. A mountain range in southwestern Idaho is named Owyhee because two Hawaiians were killed there by Indians in fur-trapping days. A Columbia River dam is named John Day because a hunter with the Astor party went mad in the area. So honoring Chea-Yow— whose murder caused international repercussions—would not be out of line.

But the purpose of this chapter is not to mount a name-changing campaign; it is to delve into a mystery that has never been solved and to speculate upon the whereabouts of a treasure that has never been found.

Writing accurately about the influx of Chinese into the American West following the discovery of gold in California is the despair of historians, for few first-hand accounts by its participants exist. Dr. Merle Wells, then archivist for the Idaho State Historical Society, once told me:

"A few years ago we did find what appeared to be a diary—written in Chinese characters, of course—and managed to get it translated. It turned out to be a grocery list."

Because most of the Chinese workers entered the United States through the port city of San Francisco, where many of the records being preserved were destroyed by fire following the great earthquake of 1906, no letters or diaries written before that date have survived. If Chinese workers lived long enough to make their fortune and return to the homeland, as many of them did, a written record of their experiences in *Gum Shan*_still existing in China would be of great interest to American historians; but so far no access to these records has been permitted.

Even in the United States, a writer delving into Chinese matters runs into roadblocks. When Marilyn Sparks, a Whitman College Library research specialist, made an inquiry for me

Idaho State Historical Society 1268-A
Chinese miners often worked claims abandoned by whites.

at the State Department a few years ago regarding a regional massacre of Chinese, an official there wrote back:

"It would be helpful if you would tell us which tribe of Indians was involved."

The word "massacre," it seems, evokes the word "Indians" even at this late date.

As it turned out, the savages who committed the "massacre" belonged to the most brutal race then extant in the West—the white race. And one of the victims was Chea-Yow.

In the Idaho gold country 100 years ago, Chinese miners were permitted to work claims only after white men had abandoned them as unprofitable. Unless the white prospector made five to ten dollars a day, he deserted the claim and sought richer diggings. But to the patient, thrifty Chinese miner, two to three dollars in flour gold was reward enough for a dawn-to-dark day of stooping, washing, and sifting.

Chea-Yow was a member of a group of ten Chinese who were working a sandbar in the depths of Hells Canyon 150 miles upstream from the spot at which his body was found.

Contrary to the impression of most Americans of that day, these were not nameless, impoverished coolies smuggled into the country and forced to work as slaves for the enrichment of their Chinese masters. Each name was recorded, each man was known, and a meticulous record of his credits and debts was kept in the office of the sponsoring company that had paid for his passage to America. The company would look after his welfare while he was here, and would either pay for his passage home or, if he died, would return his bones to the homeland for burial with those of his ancestors. For these guaranteed services, the sponsoring company took a percentage of his earnings, of course, but in no sense was he a slave.

The very word "coolie" is a corruption of "ku-li," which means "muscle strength" in the Cantonese dialect. Then, as now, "muscle strength" was the greatest resource China possessed.

The ten Chinese miners were natives of the district of Punyu, which was near Canton, and were clansmen. Their names were: Chea-Po, Chea-Sun, Chea-Yow, Chea-Shun, Chea-Cheong, Chea-Ling, Chea-Chow, Chea-Lin-Chung, Kong-Mun-Cow, and Kong-Ngan. All were members of the Sam Yup Company.

Inscrutable as Chinese ways are to Americans, one of the greatest areas of misunderstanding is the perceived difference between a benevolent Chinese "Company" and a criminal Chinese "Tong." The Six Companies, as they were called, were very much like our fraternal organizations such as the Elks, Oddfellows, and Eagles. The Tongs (sometimes called the "Triad") were criminally-oriented groups more like the Capone gang, Murder Incorporated, or the Mafia. The companies dealt in commerce; the Tongs, in crime.

Sponsored by the Sam Yup Company, the ten Chinese miners had come to *Gum Shan* in hopes of making the kind of fortune they never could have earned at home. In their distant native village, they no doubt had parents, wives, and children whose only hope for a better material existence was the gold the sojourners would send or bring home after years of privation and hard work.

With a boatload of provisions, the party arrived at Douglas Bar in the heart of Hells Canyon at the beginning of the ninth month of the Chinese twelfth year of Kwong Su—by our calendar, October, 1886.

The Snake River was running low at that season, exposing a maximum expanse of gold-bearing sand and gravel. The turbulent river acted like a gigantic sluice box, tearing loose tons of precious-metal-laden rock from the steep mountainsides of the high country, bringing the material down to the quieter reaches of the low country, then depositing it on the sandbars where, until next year's high water came, the industrious Chinese placer miners could anticipate profitable diggings.

Scenically and historically, they were working in a dramatic locale. On the Oregon side of the Snake, dark basaltic bluffs rose steeply toward the 10,000-foot peaks of the Wallowa Mountains. On the Idaho side, similar brooding slopes lifted toward the 9,500-foot crests of the Seven Devils Range.

For twenty-five years placer and hardrock miners had been stripping stream valleys, hills, and mountainsides of hundreds of millions of dollars worth of fine and coarse gold. But because of the inefficiency of their methods, each summer's flood carried new deposits down the Snake to lodge where the current slackened or eddies formed.

Just such an eddy near the bar where the Chinese were working had from time immemorial been known to the Indians of the region as one of the few places at which the Snake could be safely crossed at flood stage. It was called Nez Perce Crossing.

From the beautiful meadows, lakes, forests, and streams of the Wallowa Valley, homeland of Chief Joseph's band, a relatively easy water-level trail led down Little Sheep and Big Sheep Creek to the Imnaha River, which then was followed to the Snake.

From the Idaho side of the river, the trail wound up a series of narrow, rocky canyons, eventually leading to Lapwai, head-quarters of the much-reduced Nez Perce Indian Reservation to which the Army insisted Chief Joseph's Wallowa band move in 1877—only to precipitate a senseless war.

Joseph and his people crossed the flood-swollen Snake in June, miraculously losing no human lives and only a few animals. But even though 6,000 head of Nez Perce cattle and horses were successfully swum across the cold, treacherous river, the Army had not given the Indians time enough to round up all their livestock. So for years afterward, white men who moved into the Wallowa Country caught and claimed cattle and horses which the Indians had left behind.

Since there was little law enforcement in this remote, lightly settled part of Oregon and Idaho Territory, a breed of men euphemistically called "cowboys" began to infest the area. They rounded up stray animals left behind by the Nez Perces in Oregon, drove them to Idaho Territory, and sold them to buyers who asked no questions.

In late May, 1887, several such "cowboys" swam the river at Nez Perce Crossing, saw the ten Chinese working the bar, and began to wonder if there were not easier ways to acquire gold than by stealing livestock.

"A person named Jackson told a Chinese named Hung Ah Yee that he had witnessed some cowboys, eight in number, forcibly driving Kong Shu and his party out of the bar in their boat and throwing their provisions and bedding overboard," Chang Yen Hoon, Chinese Consul, wrote to the American Secretary of State, T. F. Bayard, some months later.

"Kong Shu and his party fled, being afraid to offer any resistance; since then, he learned of the murder of Chea-Po and nine others, and came to the conclusion that the cowboys had committed the crime. . ."

Certainly there was evidence that a crime of major proportions had been committed. During the next few weeks, bodies were found in shoals on both sides of the river, some as far downstream as Log Cabin Bar, 150 miles away, and Penawawa, ten miles below that point.

Because the waters of the Snake River are cold, the stream is slow giving up its dead. This scattering of bodies on shores under the jurisdiction of the state of Oregon and Idaho and Washington Territories caused an almost insoluble snarl of red tape.

Hearing about the murders, the Sam Yup Company sent its own investigator, Lee Loi, to Lewiston. After gathering what facts he could from Chinese in the area, he enlisted the aid of Commissioner Vincent, who also held the title of Justice of

Peace for Nez Perce County. In a curious relationship, Vincent was employed by the Sam Yup Company as a "private eye" to find out what happened, identify the guilty men, and bring them to justice. He appears to have done a good job. He wrote the Chinese Consul in San Francisco a month or so after the discovery of the murders:

> "I am still in the employ of the Chinese company, ferreting out the crime. From what I have so far found, things seem to show that white men were the murderers, as some of the provisions (taken from the Chinese miners) I have traced directly to them. I have been following up, for six days, a white man who was in their camp. . . He has told me some very curious stories. . .
>
> "But there is in that vicinity some 20 or 30 bad men and I was watched very closely for nine days. I plan to start again up the Snake River and will get into their camp by some means and know what has been done. . ."

Acting on evidence supplied by Vincent, a Wallowa County Grand Jury met, deliberated, and indicted six men on charges of murder. On April 28, 1888, the *Walla Walla Union* reported:

> "A party of men, consisting of Bruce Evans, J. T. Canfield, Homer LaRue, Robert McMillan, Carl Hughes, H. Maynard, and Frank Vaughn, entered into an agreement to murder these Chinese miners for the gold dust they thought they possessed, and agreed that if any of the party should divulge it the rest should kill him. . .
>
> "As near as we can learn, all the men except Hughes went down in the Chinese camp and opened fire on them, killing them all. . . They then secured all the money and gold dust they could find, amounting to between $4,000 and $5,000. . .
>
> "Vaughn has made a confession in accordance with the above, and we are satisfied that the matter is about straight . . . Hughes, McMillan, and Maynard have been arrested . . ."

Grand Jury proceedings cannot be revealed, I was told by a clerk, Marjorie Martin, at the Wallowa County Courthouse in Enterprise, Oregon, when my wife and I spent a morning going through the records a few years ago.

Furthermore, it was her recollection that the case never came to trial. But a bit of probing in the criminal docket proved that it did come to trial August 30, 31, and September 1, 1888. Present in person for the trial were Robert McMillan, Carl Hughes, and H. Maynard. The verdict reached by the jury and read by foreman William Green:

"Not guilty."

But the trial record, which is not privileged, is missing. This is not an uncommon happening with early-day records, for the court reporter—if there was one—often was not a county employee, took his notes home with him if he wished, then charged interested parties for a transcript in case of an appeal. At this late date, even learning the name of the reporter, let alone finding a verbatim record of the trial, is a hopeless task.

The fate of Frank Vaughn, who was reported to have told all, is not known. Nor were J. T. Canfield, Bruce Evans, and Homer LaRue ever found, though the indictment against them was kept on the court docket for several terms. But we do know what happened to Robert McMillan, who was tried and acquitted, for a few years later he made a death-bed confession admitting his part of the crime.

On September 30, 1891, the *Walla Walla Statesman* carried this report:

"On the 3rd of August last Hugh McMillan, who lives in Walla Walla and works at his trade of blacksmithing, appeared before the Hon. W. M. Clark, notary public, and made the following statement:

"'I make this statement from the statement made me by my son, Robert, aged 16, just prior to his death, and by me then reduced to writing. In the latter part of April, 1887, my son and Bruce Evans, J. T. Canfield, Mat LaRue, Frank Vaughn, Hiram Maynard and Carl Hughes were stopping in a cattle camp four miles from Snake

Idaho State Historical Society 83-37.22
Chinese encampment at Delamar, Idaho

River. My son and Evans, Canfield, LaRue and Vaughn went to the Chinese camp on Snake River. Canfield and LaRue went above the camp and Evans and Vaughn remained below.

"'There were 13 Chinese in the camp and they were fired on. Twelve Chinese were instantly killed and one other caught afterward, and his brains beaten out. The party got that evening $5,500 in gold dust. Next day eight more Chinese came to the camp in a boat. They were all killed and their bodies with the others thrown into the river. The party then took a boat and went to another Chinese camp four miles distant where 13 Chinese were working on a river bar. These were all killed and their bodies thrown into the river. The camp was robbed and $50,000 in gold secured.

"'My son was present only the first day, but was acquainted with the facts as they were talked over by the participants in his presence. The circumstances here detailed occurred on the Oregon side of the Snake River

in Wallowa County, near the northeast corner of the
state.'

"Dated Walla Walla, August 3, 1891. W. M. Clark,
Witness."

Following the quoted statement, the editor of the newspaper
commented:

"The country where the massacre occurred is in the
big canyon of the Snake near the Imnaha. It is very
inaccessible, and for the past 25 years has been the
general rendezvous of all the horse and cattle thieves of
Oregon, Idaho and Washington.

"Many bodies have, at different times, been found
bearing marks of brutal treatment. In fact, at one time
it was as much as a man's life was worth to hunt for
lost or stolen stock unless accompanied by well-armed
friends.

"The *Statesman* takes no stock in the statement that
$55,000 was realized by the murders for the reason that
rich diggings never did exist in that vicinity. Still, the
Chinese must have had considerable gold dust, as they
had been working for fully six months."

How much speculative arithmetic the editor did to reach the
conclusion that the thirty-four dead Chinese "must have had
considerable dust," we don't know. By our own calculations,
if they had averaged eight dollars a day apiece, their total
accumulation would have been a little over $52,000. But we'll
never know for sure.

What we do know is that the death-bed confession of young
Robert McMillan—which for some reason his father wished
published—raises more questions than it answers. If Robert
McMillan were sixteen years old at the time of his death in
1891, he would have been only twelve at the time he took
part in the murders. Why was a mere boy a member of such
a brutal gang?

By his account, $55,000 in gold was stolen from the Chinese.
What happened to it? Also, by his account, thirty-four Chinamen

Idaho State Historical Society 76-119.2/b
Chinese miners work a claim in the Boise Basin.

were murdered. Why were only ten listed as killed by the Sam Yup Company?

What caused Robert McMillan's death? Since this was the era of the "highbinder" and the "hatchetman," much-dreaded killers in the Chinese communities of San Francisco, Portland, Seattle, and Boise, whose trademark was a lather's hatchet left imbedded in the skull of the victim, and since his father wished to publicize the names of the other members of the gang, did the father believe that the Chinese had taken vengeance on his son and wish a similar fate would overtake them? When, where, and how did the other men eventually die?

No one knows.

But we do know that buried gold later was found at the site of the massacre. A Lewiston newspaper reported in 1902:

"A few weeks ago the tragedy was revived at Joseph, Ore., when two young men appeared there with gold dust to the amount of $700. They had been prospecting in the vicinity of the old Chinese camp and encountered the cache where the murderers had hidden the wealth, and had failed to take away the flask worth $700. . ."

What happened to the rest of the gold remains a mystery.

The massacre of the Chinese in the Snake River country was but one of many acts of brutality committed by whites against Orientals during the 1880s. In California alone, the Chinese Consul wrote the State Department, an estimated 100,000 of his countrymen were deprived of their property and driven from their homes. In a token gesture, the American government agreed October 19, 1888:

"To pay, out of humane consideration, and without reference to the question of liability therefore, the sum of $276,619.75 to the Chinese government as full indemnity for all the losses and injuries sustained by Chinese subjects within the United States at the hands of residents thereof."

In view of the fact that since 1850 China had been America's best Asian friend—and would remain a friend for many years to come—the "humane consideration" seems minuscule indeed.

But Chea-Yow, at least, lies buried under an impressive tombstone—a $298 million dam.

May his spirit rest in peace.

12

HANK VAUGHAN
THE AMIABLE HORSE THIEF

In the small town of Athena, Oregon, a few miles north of Pendleton, no statue has been erected in honor of its most infamous citizen, Hank Vaughan. But the region's folklorist, Russell Blankenship, writes that back in the 1930s, local people pointed with pride at the bullet marks in the walls and the hoof scars in the floors of several saloons in Athena and the nearby town of Adams into which Hank Vaughan used to ride his horse and shoot off his guns while on a drunken spree.

On one occasion when a saloon patron protested the intrusion of the rider and his horse, Hank is said to have demanded, "Well, what are you doin' in here afoot, anyway?" Local people claim that Hank never hurt anybody during his sprees; when he sobered up next day, he always returned and paid for the damage he had done.

Like many other young men back in the 1880s, Hank's fondness for fast horses and strong drink often got him in trouble. Running free on the nearby Umatilla Indian Reservation were thousands of tough, sure-footed ponies, a breed so renowned for its stamina that the name of the tribe that raised it, the Cayuse Indians, became generic for the most durable kind of horse in the West. More than one teen-ager seeking to make a quick buck found it easy to round up a few dozen horses from the unfenced bunch-grass hills and hollows of the reservation, drive them across the Blue Mountains to Idaho, then sell them to ranchers who asked no questions.

At the age of eighteen, Hank and an older man named Dan Burns put together a herd of stolen horses and started driving them across the mountains, intending to sell them in Boise. Informed of the theft, Umatilla County Sheriff Frank Maddock and Deputy O. J. Hart got on the trail of the thieves and tracked them to the Baker area. Hearing that the fugitives were camped on Burnt River, Sheriff Maddock did not bother enlisting a posse to help him, for he knew he had only two people to arrest, one of them a teen-ager.

It was well after dark when Maddock and Hart reached the camp of the horse thieves. Dismounting some distance from the spot where the two men were sleeping, the officers approached warily, the sheriff whispering to his deputy,

"You cover the boy. I'll take care of the man."

This proved to be a fatal mistake. When Deputy Hart jerked the blankets off the sleeping men and yelled, "Law officers! You're under arrest!" both of them came up shooting. In the ensuing gunfight, outlaw Dan Burns and Deputy Sheriff O. J. Hart were killed, while Hank Vaughan and Sheriff Frank Maddock were wounded.

After Maddock fell, Vaughan, whose gun was empty, beat him over the head with the butt of his pistol, then hopped on a saddled horse and rode off into the night. In the nearby camp of miners through which the law officers had passed the previous afternoon on the trail of the horse thieves, friends who knew their mission grew alarmed when they did not return with their prisoners, formed a posse, and followed their trail down Burnt River. Soon they came to the camp where the gunfight had taken place, found the two dead men and the unconscious sheriff, who appeared to be dying. While one group cared for the casualties the other trailed Hank Vaughan, whose wound was so disabling he could not travel fast or far.

Found and captured with no more gunplay, Vaughan was taken to Auburn, the nearby county seat, and placed in jail to await trial. Popular indignation at the killing of one law officer and the apparently fatal wounding of another reached such a fevered pitch that a band of vigilantes soon formed and marched on the jail, intent on hanging the prisoner. But the way was blocked by a well-known local citizen named John Hailey, who stood in the jail door with a pistol in each hand.

"The prisoner will be tried by a regular court," he announced firmly. "Anybody who thinks otherwise will have to get past me."

Because John Hailey was respected for both his integrity and his skill with firearms, the mob backed off, complaining that somebody was always spoiling their fun. Writing about the event many years later, Russell Blankenship agreed:

> "John Hailey was a public spirited and courageous man, but his public spirit and courage were put to a sorry use that day in Auburn. If he had simply gone about his business, the state of Oregon would have been spared the outlay of many thousands for court and prison expenses, the Northwest would have saved untold thousands in loot, and society would have profited immeasurably."

Maybe so. But if that had happened, this chapter would not have been written, for the colorful career of Hank Vaughan had just begun.

Even though a bullet from Hank's gun passed through the skull of Sheriff Maddock, destroyed the inner ear, then emerged from the back of the head, the officer survived to testify at Vaughan's trial. Though reasonably sure that Hank had fired the bullet that killed Deputy Hart, the sheriff could not prove the assumption beyond a shadow of a doubt. So in view of his youth and lack of a previous criminal record, instead of being hanged as he probably deserved to be, Hank Vaughan was sentenced to eight years in the Oregon State Penitentiary.

While doing his prison time, Hank seems to have learned two useful things: (1) the blacksmith trade; and (2) not to get caught the next time he committed a crime.

Returning to the Pendleton area following his release from prison, Hank found an occupation that suited him better than blacksmithing—marrying a widow woman with enough Indian blood in her veins to have inherited a large, productive wheat ranch on the reservation. The ranch could be worked by the woman's husky sons while Hank devoted his time and energy to more interesting pursuits such as drinking, racing horses, and an occasional bit of hell-raising.

Whether his newly-acquired wife kept Hank in funds or he acquired spending money by other means, is not known. But he always seemed to have enough cash on hand to buy a few drinks, purchase a few spirited horses, and pay the damage bill when he went on a spree and wrecked the interior of a saloon. A few local people did notice that he went on a trip now and then to unannounced destinations and while he was gone, a train, a bank, or a business establishment in a distant community was held up by a small-statured, wiry bandit about Hank's size. When Hank came home he spent money more freely than usual. But if any of these local people connected Hank's absence or size to these distant events, they were careful to keep such speculations to themselves.

"Hank was a fancier of horse-flesh and an expert driver and rider," Russell Blankenship writes. "As the old-timers around Pendleton say, he could drive a six-horse team where most men would be afraid to drag a halter-rope."

Not long after Hank Vaughan returned to his former haunts, a kindred soul moved into the area. Calling himself Doc Whitley, the newcomer said he came from Arizona; beyond that, he told nothing about himself or his background. Rumor had it that he had been involved in the Earp-Clanton feud in Tombstone, and that, when the gunsmoke cleared over the O.K Corral, he came north for his health, finding the eastern Oregon air of Adams more salubrious than that of the desert Southwest.

Opening a saloon on Main Street, which soon became the favorite hangout for a number of ill-favored local citizens, Doc Whitley was not long in finding Hank Vaughan his best customer and closest friend. Together, the two men made a lot of lively local history.

One day Hank, who had downed a few drinks, drove up to the saloon behind a team of feisty young horses hitched to a light buggy. Coming out on the porch, Doc Whitley, who was also well-lubricated, eyed the rig critically, then observed,

"Pears to me like you're scared of your team, Hank. Why don't you hire a man to break them for you?"

"Hop in and I'll take you for a ride," Hank grunted. "If you're man enough to do the job, you can help me break 'em."

According to Blankenship:

"Doc jumped into the buggy, seized the whip, and poured the lash to the horses. Dare-devil Hank, instead of trying to control the team, threw the lines to the ground and gave an Indian yell. The runaway was one of the most successful that Adams ever saw. Down the street the team dashed pell-mell, Doc whipping the horses and Hank yelling. The team was going much too fast to make a turn, and the frantic horses, the smashed buggy, and the men all ended up in a heap beside the road. Doc and Hank were so severely injured that for a few days hope was entertained for their demise, but the reckless devils were too wiry. Hank survived to plague the community for years."

In appearance, Hank was a small, inoffensive-looking man, well-mannered, with a gift for pleasant conversation when sober. When drunk, he became a wild man. The one crude picture of him that has survived shows him to be a small man with short chin whiskers which gave him the sedate look of a frontier preacher. He was in the habit of wearing a Prince Albert coat, people who knew him said, not so much to accentuate his ministerial appearance but to hide the two six-shooters he always carried in his belt and could draw with lightning speed. Aspiring badmen who crossed Hank's trail found that the solemn garb concealed both the firearms and the uncertain temper of a mountain thunderstorm.

Hank also was very sensitive to published remarks about his career and business. On one occasion, the editor of the *Pendleton East Oregonian*, John P. Wager, printed a news item that informed the paper's readers that, "Hank Vaughan, the gambler, is reported dead."

According to Blankenship:

"The report was slightly inaccurate and distinctly premature. Vaughan was not famous for his gambling, nor was he dead. By way of correcting the gross inaccuracy and rebuking Wager's editorial carelessness, Hank rode to Pendleton, descended on the *East Oregonian* office waving a gun, and sent editor, reporters, printers, and printer's devil skipping into the street."

When things got dull around Athena, Hank liked to liven them up by spurring his horse into first one saloon and then another, paying his respects to the bartenders and having a drink in every bar, then riding his horse up and down the street, firing his pistol at random. Speculating on why some local law officer or law-abiding citizen did not fill Hank's hide with a load of buckshot, Blankenship mused that they probably knew if their first shot missed, Hank's would not, for he "had a habit of collecting dividends on the first bullet."

People who knew him say that Hank seldom picked on a tenderfoot as a victim of his waggish pranks. His favorite pastime was to walk into a saloon where some would-be bad-man was bragging about his deeds. After listening for a while without comment until the loudmouth paused for breath, Hank would draw a pistol and say, "You've proved what a great talker you are, friend. Now show us how well you can dance."

As musical accompaniment to the two-step, the jig, or whatever other latest step the entertainer decided to perform, Hank would beat time on the bar with the barrel of his six-shooter. Now and then he added a bit of excitement by shooting a bullet or two into the floor between the performer's feet.

"While the dancers may have lacked the grace of Nijinski," Blankenship says, "their exhibitions were staged with admirable verve. More than a few responded with encores."

But on one occasion—which would become legend in the town—Hank made a mistake. Finding no braggart visiting the saloon that particular day, he chose as his premier *danseur* a stranger to Athena, a mild-looking, unarmed man who was quietly enjoying a drink and boasting to no one. Feeling in need of a little diversion, Hank drew his forty-four and rapped on the bar to get the stranger's attention.

"Tell me, friend. Can you do the mazurka?"

"Sorry," the man said politely. "I'm not much of a dancer."

"Well, give it a try, anyway. I'll play the tune."

As Hank fired bullets into the floor near the stranger's feet, they began to move in a lively fashion. But some of the local bar patrons noticed that the glint in the man's eyes did not seem to be born of abject terror. Satisfied with the quality and quantity of the dancing, Hank told the man he could quit, holstered his gun, left the saloon, and wandered into a nearby dry-goods store to buy some items he had promised to pick up for his wife. The stranger also left the bar, going into a hardware store across the street, where he bought a pistol and a box of shells. Then he went looking for his recent dance instructor.

Finding Hank in the dry-goods store leaning against a spool-case with his back to the door, the stranger raised his pistol and began shooting. The first shot went through the spool-case and broke Hank's right arm. Vaughan's only weakness as a gunfighter at that time, Blankenship says, was his lack of ambidexterity. He shot exclusively with his right hand. With his pistol arm broken, all Hank could do was crouch behind the spool-case and wait for the bombardment to subside. When the hammer at last clicked on an empty shell, the stranger left the store and the community—never to be seen again. To this day, his identity is unknown. Blankenship says:

"In addition to the shot which broke his arm, Hank collected two or three other bullets in various portions of his body, none, however, in a vital spot. The gaping crowd, which came on a gallop at the sound of gunfire, counted six holes in the spool-case. For a tenderfoot handling a brand-new pistol with which he had not practiced, the unknown marksman did some pretty fancy shooting. So fancy, indeed, that Athena was convinced that it had entertained a celebrity unaware."

One of Doc Whitley's former friends or enemies from Tombstone, perhaps? Wyatt Earp? Doc Holliday? Wild Bill

Hickock? Maybe even Calamity Jane herself, who was said to travel disguised as a man? Would it be possible to stage a re-match?

Local gunfighter fans never knew. But Hank Vaughan had learned his lesson. If he were to succeed or even survive in his chosen trade, he had better learn how to shoot as well with his left hand as he did with his right.

A few days later, a Pendleton lawyer needing Hank's signature on some legal papers dropped by the family residence, sure that this time he would find the head of the household at home. A step-daughter who answered the door said that Hank was upstairs in bed. Showing the visitor to the foot of the stairs, she cautioned him,

"Make sure he knows you're coming. He's practicing."

"Practicing what?"

"Shooting left-handed. He says it's something he's always wanted to learn. Laid up like he is, he thinks now is a good time to practice."

Making a lot of noise as he tramped up the stairs, the lawyer cautiously peeked around the door. Hank was propped up in bed, shooting with his left hand at a playing card pinned to the opposite wall.

"Hank was delighted to have a visitor," Blankenship writes. "He explained that his right arm might not be steady for some time and that he wished to make the most of his enforced idleness by improving his skill with his left hand. That was Hank, always eager to perfect himself in the technique of his chosen profession."

Following his recovery, Hank decided to show off his newly acquired proficiency as a two-handed gunman by staging a shooting contest in an Athena bar. After having a few drinks with a group of his rowdy friends, he proposed a game.

"We'll each have a drink," he said. "When we've emptied our glasses, we'll set 'em on the bar, go to the other side of the room, draw and fire. Whoever misses his glass has to buy the next round."

Everybody present thought that was a great idea—except the bartender, who was not consulted. Though assured of an immediate increase in business, he doubted it would be worth it. After serving and collecting for a round of drinks, the bartender found it prudent to drop flat on the floor behind the bar, lie there until the crash of gunfire ended, then rise and serve another round. How long the competition lasted and who had to buy the most drinks, has not been recorded. But it is known that Hank returned to the saloon, next day, and cheerfully paid the damage bill, which amounted to several hundred dollars.

One of the local legends attached to Hank's name was the way he acquired a lifetime pass on the recently completed Northern Pacific Railroad. Returning to Pendleton from a trip to Spokane with his wife, Hank sat dozing in the day coach when his nap was interrupted by a group of robbers who had boarded the train at its last stop. Bursting into the car with drawn revolvers, their leader yelled,

"This is a stickup! All you men, put up your hands! Ladies, get ready to give us your purses and your jewelry!"

Caught dozing, Hank had no choice but to obey. Getting to his feet and raising his hands while his wife remained seated beside him, he watched helplessly as the robbers moved along the aisle, collecting watches, billfolds, and purses from the passengers as they progressed. As usual when traveling, he was dressed in his long Prince Albert coat, under which he wore two holstered guns. With the bandits still a few feet away, he murmured to his wife,

"Reach under my coat and unbuckle my belt. Then drop to the floor."

Without asking any foolish questions, Mrs. Vaughan did as she was told. As the gunbelt and six-shooters dropped clear of his coat-tails, Hank reached down, caught their grips, then came up shooting. The lead bandit fell dead on the spot, while the others fled cravenly, so surprised that they did not fire a shot. Caught, arrested, charged, and tried, they were convicted and put out of circulation for a long time. In gratitude for his bravery, the Northern Pacific Railroad gave Hank Vaughan a lifetime pass on which he could ride free anywhere their trains ran. Blankenship noted:

"Umatilla County buzzed over the incident for years. Hank, it was uncharitably charged, was not so much exercised over a breach of law as he was over unfair competition . . . He was very wroth to find utter strangers poaching on his domain."

Though widely recognized as the Resident Badman of Northeast Oregon, Hank did venture out of his territory on one occasion to test his talents against a rival. In Central Oregon 200 miles to the west, a man named Charlie Long had established himself as Champion Badman of the John Day, Deschutes River region. Learning that Long's favorite hangout was a saloon in Prineville, Hank decided to make a pilgrimage there and see what his competitor was made of.

Reaching Prineville after a dusty three-day ride, Hank had no difficulty locating Charlie Long in his favorite saloon, introduced himself, and said he would like to buy Long a drink. Well aware of Vaughan's reputation and his reason for making the trip, Long accepted. Blankenship describes the encounter:

"The two stood at the bar and sized each other up with appraising eyes, both excessively polite but also excessively cautious. After the drink Hank politely suggested a game of cards. The two considerately went out on the porch. By way of starting the game of seven-up with the proper tone, Long drew his Bowie knife and pinned Hank's leather chaps to the floor. Vaughan, unwilling to lag behind in an exhibition of savoir faire, did the same with Long's chaps. After a hand or two Long leaned over and said, 'Hank, you'd make a good cannoneer in hell.' Hank retorted in kind, and the reverberation of pistol shots shook the air of the little village. When the smoke cleared away, the two gunmen lay unconscious. The somewhat bored citizens of Prineville picked them up, put them to bed in the same room but in different beds, summoned a doctor, and went about their affairs, cheerfully hoping for the best. They were a bit discouraged the next day to discover that both duelists were recovering."

A few days later, local legend relates, Hank Vaughan regained consciousness, weakly raised himself on one elbow, and looked at the other bed. In it lay Charlie Long, who also had become aware of his surroundings.

"Charlie," Hank said, "they oughtn't to waste two beds on a couple of damn fools like us. Lay over."

So saying, he tottered across the room and went to bed with his late opponent, a move regarded as such a fine sporting gesture that it completely won Charlie Long's heart.

In fact, Long was so impressed that several years later, when he heard that Hank had been seriously injured by an accident not related to his profession as a gunfighter, he journeyed to Pendleton. He was devastated by the news that Hank's condition was so serious he was not allowed to have visitors. Mentally debating what to do, Charlie dropped into a local saloon, had a few drinks, then shared his problem with a sympathetic bartender, who said,

"Maybe you ought to send him some flowers."

A great idea, Charlie agreed, then was deeply disappointed to find that there were no florist shops in Pendleton and that in the summer's heat no roses, daffodils, carnations or other appropriate flowers were blooming in any local gardens. So he went back to the saloon and had another drink or two, while he pondered on what to do.

As he stood staring out the dusty window, a well-dressed lady wearing a fancy hat decorated with a colorful array of artificial flowers passed along the boardwalk. The solution to his problem struck him like a bolt from the blue.

"Three more drinks in quick succession suffused Charlie with the glow of plenary inspiration," according to Blankenship. "Weaving unsteadily, he went to the only millinery store in town, bought its entire stock of artificial flowers, and sent them to assuage Hank's wounded body and spirit. Then, brimming full of liquor and self-esteem, he rode back to his bailiwick in Central Oregon."

Some months later, Vaughan turned down another chance to meet his rival from Prineville. Hank was sitting in an Athena saloon, with his chair tipped back against the wall. The bartender, who was standing at the door looking out at the street, saw a familiar figure riding by.

"Hey, Hank, there goes your friend, Charlie Long. Did you know he was in town?"

Hank did not answer or move.

"Don't you want to see him?" the bartender persisted.

"No," Hank grunted wearily. "I seen him once."

Hank Vaughan came to the end of his colorful career on a warm summer day in 1893. Ironically, it was the arrival of civilization that proved to be his undoing. According to Blankenship:

"By that time Pendleton was showing signs of progress, at least to the extent that it had telephone poles in the streets and one piece of concrete sidewalk. On a June day of that year Hank rode his cayuse to Pendleton evidently with the intention of reminding the town of its boisterous youth. Filling himself with whiskey, he mounted his horse and charged up and down the streets in his usual fashion. But, alas, the stars had determined aeons before that Hank and progress were not to be congenial fellow travelers. The horse slipped on the one piece of concrete sidewalk in eastern Oregon, and Hank's skull was fractured against a telephone pole."

Wooden barroom floors, the horse could handle. But not a concrete sidewalk.

His skull fractured beyond repair, Hank lingered unconscious for a week while three doctors, including a surgeon brought up from Portland, tried to save him. But their efforts failed. When he died, the editor of the *East Oregonian* wrote a fitting tribute:

"Ah, Hank, that was a fateful ride, the last time you mounted your trusty sorrel in the streets of Pendleton and sped with him like a tempest until his sure feet could not keep pace with your impetuosity and you were plunged headlong upon the rocks.:

The editor of *The Dalles Mountaineer* also wrote a tribute to the Northeast Oregon Badman:

"Vaughan, although having somewhat of the character of a desperado in his early life, has many warm friends in this part of the state who will be pained to hear of his passing."

This time, the subject of the news stories did not come storming into the editorial offices to dispute their accuracy.

As a footnote to this chapter, we would like to add a couple of Hank Vaughan tales told to us years ago by local old-timers about their encounters with the outlaw which we are sure have never been published in book form before.

In the first story, a farmer and his wife and children were driving across the dusty foothills five or six miles south of Walla Walla when a piece of harness hitching the team to the wagon broke, leaving them stranded. As the farmer pondered what to do, Hank Vaughan came galloping along the road, reined in, and inquired,

"What's your problem, friend?"

"The team's harness broke," the farmer said, holding up the broken pieces of leather. "Now we're stuck."

"Aw, that's easy to fix," Hank said, swinging down out of the saddle. Going to a nearby barb-wire fence, he snipped out a ten-inch piece with a pair of pliers, worried holes with a pocket knife in the sections of broken leather harness, and then spliced them together. "There, that oughta do you," he grunted, hopped back on his horse, and galloped away.

Ever since that time, local legend says, using barbed wire to repair a broken harness has been called "the Hank Vaughan hitch."

In the other tale, a ten-year-old boy named Will Sterling, who would eventually grow up to become a substantial citizen of the area, was working as a sheepherder in the foothills of the Blue Mountains when a small, wiry, mustached man came riding hell-for-leather across the country. Noticing that the boy had a coffee pot simmering over the campfire, the man reined in, then, after taking a long look at his back-trail and finding it empty for the moment, peered down at the boy and asked,

"Can you spare me a cup of coffee, son?"

Being a friendly sort of youngster and eager to have some company, Will invited the stranger to light and sip. Ground-tying his lathered mount by dropping its reins to the ground, the stranger hunkered down by the camp fire and poured himself a cup of coffee, still keeping a wary eye on his back-trail as he drank it.

He was wearing an expensive pair of holstered Colt revolvers, Will noticed, which the boy thought were very handsome. Finding the gunbelt uncomfortable in this position, the stranger unbuckled it and laid it on the ground.

Being young and unfamiliar with the customs of the county, the boy gazed admiringly at the bone-handled, silver-encrusted pistols, then impulsively reached out and took one of them out of its holster. The next thing he knew his forearm was clamped in a grip of steel.

"What d'ye think you're doing, son?"

"I was only curious, sir," Will apologized in embarrassment. "I've never seen such fancy guns."

Retrieving the six-shooter and putting it back in its holster before he relaxed his grip on the boy's arm, the stranger said softly, "Boy, when you grow up—if you ever do—you can tell your grandchildren that you're the only person in the world that ever took a gun away from Hank Vaughan and lived to brag about it."

Finishing his coffee, the stranger mounted his horse and galloped away. Ten minutes later, half a dozen grim-faced horsemen rode into the camp, led by a man who wore a star.

"Did Hank Vaughan come by here?" the sheriff demanded.

Re-telling the story to his grand-children many years later, a much older, much wiser Will Sterling said it did not occur to him to say, "Yes, he did. I took a gun away from him, then gave it back. He went thataway."

As a matter of fact, Will said, he was too speechless even to point.

13

HARRY ORCHARD
MINERS' UNION HIT MAN

Frank Steunenberg, well-to-do businessman, sheep rancher, and former governor of Idaho, had recently been
converted to his wife's religious faith, the Seventh Day
Adventist Church. That was why he postponed until after dark
that Saturday evening, December 30, 1905, walking downtown
and closing a business transaction, for the Adventist Sabbath
lasted from sunset Friday until sunset Saturday.

The Steunenberg residence was located on the southeast
outskirts of Caldwell, Idaho, about a mile from the Saratoga
Hotel, whose lobby was the usual after-hours meeting place
for the town's businessmen and ranchers. At that time,
Caldwell boasted a population of about 1,100. Boise City,
twenty-five miles to the east, claimed some 18,000 residents,
the statehouse, the penitentiary, and a brand new electric
trolley line.

A light skiff of snow covered the ground and holiday candles
flickered in many windows. After chatting with friends for
half an hour or so in the lobby of the Saratoga Hotel, Frank
Steunenberg walked homeward through the early winter darkness. Somewhere along the way, he must have met a chunky,
out-of-breath man hurrying in the opposite direction. The man
had been watching his movements for weeks, and now, taking

advantage of this golden opportunity, had hastily deposited a package at the ex-governor's gate, rigged it with practiced skill, and then scuttled for town.

When Steunenberg opened the gate, there was a terrific explosion. Badly mangled, he was carried into his bedroom where in the presence of his wife, son, and a neighbor he died within half an hour.

The quiet little town of Caldwell was thrown into an uproar. Method and motive seemed clear. The method—a bomb. The motive—revenge. All exit and entry to Caldwell was rigidly controlled. Messages were dispatched to Governor Frank R. Gooding in Boise. A special train was immediately made up in the capital and started toward Caldwell, loaded with state officials and law officers. Every stranger became a suspect . . .

The assassination of Frank Steunenberg in 1905 set off a series of events so far-reaching and bizarre that they made headlines for years. Steunenberg, a Democrat and a staunch union man, had been Governor of Idaho in 1899 when labor troubles developed in the Couer d'Alene mining district in the northern part of the state. Among the mines struck by newly-formed Western Federation of Miners Union was the giant Bunker Hill & Sullivan, one of the richest mines in the West. When the owners refused to recognize the union or give in to its demands, a mob of 1,000 miners, many of them masked, commandeered a train, loaded it with a ton of explosives, went to the mine building, and blew it to smithereens. In the fracas, two mine guards were killed by gunfire.

Having helped elect Steunenberg, who was viewed as sympathetic toward labor, the more radical of the union leaders thought they had him in their pocket and that he would do nothing. But as governor of Idaho, he felt he had to act—and did. When the state militia proved inadequate to restore order, he called for federal help. United States troops, many of them Negroes, moved in; hundreds of union miners were arrested and held for months in a "bullpen;" the union was broken so far as the Coeur d'Alene country was concerned; and Frank Steunenberg became an enemy of labor.

Now, six years later, he had been disposed of—and the

consensus was that a Western Federation of Miners paid bomb man had done the job . . .

Governor Frank Gooding; James Hawley, Idaho's foremost attorney; and William Borah, newly chosen U.S. Senator, were close friends of the Steunenberg family. All of them pledged their personal resources and those of the state to the task of tracking down and convicting the killer.

A prime suspect was soon found. A chunky, round-faced man who went by the name of Thomas Hogan, claimed to be a sheep-buyer, and was registered at the Saratoga Hotel. A

Idaho State Historical Society 503-8
Frank Steunenberg

search of Hogan's room turned up plaster of Paris, a piece of fish-line, acid residue in an empty bottle, a powder-stained coat pocket, and other tools of the bomb-maker's trade. He was arrested, jailed, and questioned. But he stuck to his story—he was a sheep-buyer, nothing more.

In those days, investigations of major crimes often were turned over to professional private agencies, such as the Thiel Detective Service or the Pinkerton Agency. The first professional on the scene was Captain Swain from the Spokane office of the Thiel Agency. Governor Gooding hired him to take charge of sweating the truth out of Thomas Hogan.

Among the papers that have survived in the files of the Idaho Historical Society are the confidential reports of Captain Swain and his operatives to the governor. These cover the several weeks that the Thiel Agency was involved in the investigation. If bright lights, rubber hoses, or strong-arm methods of persuasion were used on the suspect, they were not detailed.

Thomas Hogan stuck to his story: he was nothing but a sheep-buyer, incriminated by circumstantial evidence. He had

Idaho State Historical Society 71-84.2
When Frank Steunenberg opened the gate outside his Caldwell, Idaho
home, he was mortally wounded by an assassin's bomb.

been using the plaster of Paris to make a set of loaded dice,
he swore. The fish-line was for fishing. He knew nothing about
the Western Federation of Miners.

Yet strangely enough, shortly after Thomas Hogan's arrest
and without his sending a message to anyone, a telegram
arrived from Fred Miller, in Spokane, saying that he was
heading for Caldwell to defend Hogan. Miller was an attorney
for the Western Federation of Miners. From the Denver
headquarters of the Federation, William Haywood, Executive
Secretary, sent an urgent telegram to the union miners in
Silver City, Idaho, directly south of Caldwell, urging the local
to raise a defense fund for Hogan. The message was turned up
by a Thiel operative, who had become a member of the union.
The Silver City local declined to have anything to do with
defending a man who appeared to have murdered ex-Governor
Steunenberg.

After going along with Captain Swain and the Thiel Agency
for several weeks, Gooding, Hawley, and Borah felt it was
time for a change. Governor Gooding wired James McParland,
Western manager of the Pinkerton Detective Agency in Denver,
asking him if he would take charge of the case. McParland
wired back, "Catching next train to Boise."

James McParland was a man of bulldog tenacity, tough, fearless, intelligent, and a master of psychology. Thirty years earlier he had made himself a national reputation for his work in breaking up a radical labor organization called the "Molly McGuires" in the Pennsylvania coal fields. A young man in his twenties then, his method had been to pose as a miner under the assumed name of Frank McKenna. He worked, drank, and caroused with the violent element until he had gained its confidence, then exposed the guilty parties in a series of trials that sent a number of men to the gallows.

Idaho State Historical Society 60-I.I.225
Harry Orchard

To union men, McParland was the devil incarnate. To capitalists, he was the white knight in armor. In 1906, he was in his late fifties, not in the best of health, ponderous, slow, and sparing of speech. But what he lacked in physical vitality he more than made up for in mental capacity and experience. When he moved in on a case, he supervised every detail; he played rough and he played for keeps. But so did the other side.

During the eighteen months between the day of his first employment by the state of Idaho and the time when the case finally went to trial, McParland made almost daily written confidential reports to Governor Gooding. This record runs over 1,000 pages and gives a fascinating insight into the workings of the mind of the greatest detective of that day.

McParland's first act upon reaching Boise and conferring with Governor Gooding, Hawley, and Borah was to tell them that he could not work with the Thiel Agency in any way. He trusted no one but his own operatives. He appears to have had a professional contempt for Captain Swain, discrediting everything the rival detective had done, even suggesting that the Thiel man had switched sides and now was secretly working for the defense.

The crime was committed in Caldwell, Canyon County, but as it had outgrown the capabilities of a rural sheriff and prosecutor, McParland suggested the prisoner, Thomas Hogan, be transferred from the Caldwell jail to the state penitentiary at Boise, in adjoining Ada County. Even in a case of such importance, toes must not be stepped on politically; sheriffs, judges, and county prosecutors must be pacified. With McParland calling the moves behind the scenes, Governor Gooding arranges for the transfer of the prisoner. As special prosecutors for the state, he appoints James Hawley and William Borah.

Now McParland goes to work on the prisoner. First, he tells Warden Whitney to put Thomas Hogan alone in a comfortable but isolated cell and ban all visitors and no news of any kind for several days. The idea is to make Hogan feel completely deserted. After a few days, McParland pays the prisoner a visit without revealing his identity. He tells the prisoner that the evidence against him is ironclad; that if brought to trial, he is bound to be convicted and hanged; and that the people who hired him to assassinate the ex-Governor regard him as expendable and will not lift a finger to help him.

Without making any specific promises of leniency, McParland then goes on to say he feels sorry for the prisoner; that he knows he is merely a tool; that others conspired with him; that the big men should suffer rather than him. McParland expounds at some length on similar cases in other parts of the country, particularly the Molly McGuires, where the hirelings who committed the actual crimes turned state's evidence and got off scot-free. McParland also touches on the religious side of things, pointing out that the worst of sinners can be forgiven if he confesses his sins.

The prisoner, Thomas Hogan, listens attentively and politely. He requests time to think it over, and asks McParland to come back and see him soon.

A few days later, McParland pays the prisoner a second visit and talks to him in the same vein. Now the prisoner recognizes him as the famous detective, James McParland, is flattered and awed, and again asks for time to think it over. Shortly thereafter, the Hogan sends word to McParland that he is ready to make a full confession. . .

The confession dictated to the prison stenographer during the next few days covers some 200 typewritten pages. The prisoner's real name is Albert Horsley, he says, though since coming west from Ontario, Canada, some years ago he has usually gone by the name Harry Orchard. That is the name he prefers now. He is a bigamist, a wife-stealer, an arsonist, a cheater at dice and cards, and has played a leading role in the murder of at least twenty men. But now he has seen the light; he has repented; he wants to get right with God. And McParland has shown him the way.

Most important to McParland is the fact that the Harry Orchard confession has revealed the names of the big shots behind him. They are: Charles Moyer, president of the Western Federation of Miners; William Haywood, executive secretary; George Pettibone, former W.F.A. treasurer; and Jack Simpkins, executive board member.

Talking it over with Governor Gooding, Hawley, and Borah, McParland points out that the above-named men are the real murderers and the prosecution should go after them, rather than their tool, Harry Orchard. They agree. He has a plan, that he outlines to them . . .

According to Idaho law, any person or persons who conspire to commit a murder—no matter where the conspiring is done—are considered to be present in fact when the murder is committed. Idaho law does not recognize an accessory before the fact; an accomplice is regarded to be as much of a principal as the killer himself.

In his confession, Harry Orchard has sworn that he was hired and instructed to assassinate Steunenberg by Charles Moyer, William Haywood, George Pettibone, and Jack Simpkins. The conspiring took place in Denver some months before the murder, and the first three men named were *in* Denver when the bomb went off.

No matter, McParland points out. They conspired; murder

was committed; therefore, they were present in the eyes of the law. Thus, they are extraditable from the State of Colorado to the state of Idaho, where they must answer for their crime. Gooding, Hawley, and Borah agree. So when the proper time comes, McParland says, we'll extradite them, bring them to Idaho, and try them for murder. But there are other matters to attend to first.

In his confession, Harry Orchard has stated that Jack Simpkins, member of the executive board of the Western Federation of Miners, came to Idaho with him, helped him shadow Steunenberg, and then moved on before the murder was committed. It certainly may be assumed that Jack Simpkins was in Idaho when the bomb went off. Wherever he is now, he must be found and tried, too. But Jack Simpkins has disappeared, and all the efforts of the far-flung Pinkerton system can find no trace of him. However, his wife, who lives in Spokane, is under constant watch, and sooner or later must give away his whereabouts.

In his confession, Harry Orchard states that a man named Steve Adams was with him and assisted him on many of his bombing missions, not the least of which was the bombing of the Independence, Colorado, railroad depot, where some fourteen non-union scabs were blown into eternity. According to Idaho law, the confession of an admitted murderer cannot be used to convict other members of the conspiracy—unless it can be corroborated by "independent evidence." Steve Adams, according to Harry Orchard, is a habitual drunk, a weakling, and an ignorant man. If he can be found and arrested, a master psychologist like James McParland no doubt can wring a confession out of him in short order, if he gets the idea that by confessing he can save his own neck. Governor Gooding, Hawley, and Borah agree that the State of Idaho can make no promises in advance; still, there are ways to get the message across.

Time is running on. Jack Simpkins and Steve Adams cannot be found. Almost daily, McParland is conferring with Harry Orchard, who now is the most willing and eager of witnesses, on details of his confession, seeking to pin down "independent evidence" to corroborate it. Orchard's trail of violence is a long and crooked one, beginning at the Bunker Hill & Sullivan mill explosion in northern Idaho in 1899 and wandering with little rhyme or reason across the states of Washington, Oregon, California, Montana, and Wyoming. But always, Orchard claims, as a paid killer for the Western Federation of Miners.

Reluctantly, McParland agrees to go ahead with Simpkins and Adams still missing. Down in Denver, Charles Moyer, Bill Haywood, and George Pettibone are getting nervous; they know something is being cooked up, and the lack of news worries them. Fred Miller, the W.F.M. attorney from Spokane, is in Boise, conferring frequently with Harry Orchard and trying to set up his defense. Miller does not know that Orchard has confessed and that every word said by him to Miller is quickly passed on to McParland. Moyer is ill and acting queerly; Haywood no longer trusts him.

Haywood is the driving force on the executive board. He is tough, aggressive and smart. His early years as a miner were spent in Silver City, Idaho, fifty miles south of the gate where Steunenberg died. He lost the sight of his left eye in a childhood accident and does not like to be approached from his blind side. He favors merging the Western Federation of Miners with the radical Industrial Workers of the World, which plans to end the conflict between capital and labor by taking over the means of production—by bloody revolution, if necessary. At least that's what the enemies of the I.W.W. claim—and the tone of the more radical labor papers bears out the theory.

Now McParland moves into action. He writes a confidential letter to Governor McDonald of Colorado. He writes another to Colorado Supreme Court Justice Goddard. He tells them he has something of importance to talk to them about, says he will be in Denver shortly, and begs for a few minutes of their valuable time.

Before leaving Boise, McPharland goes over his plan in detail with Gooding, Hawley, and Borah. A code system is set up so that they may communicate with one another by telegram and letter without the enemy catching on to what they are saying, in case the messages are intercepted. Code name for McParland will be "Owl." Hawley is "Fox." Borah is

"Wolf." Idaho and Colorado towns are given southern names such as "Savannah" and "Mobile" so that they cannot be identified by persons not in the know. Moyer is "Rattler." Haywood is "Viper."

McParland goes to Denver and has a talk with Supreme Court Justice Goddard. In this session, Harry Orchard's confession is read aloud. At one point in his confession, Harry Orchard states that a year or so earlier the Western Federation of Miners employed him to assassinate Colorado Supreme Court Justice Gabbart. Orchard was to plant a bomb in a hole next to a path in a vacant lot Judge Gabbert customarily crossed each morning. A purse would be attached to a wire triggering the bomb. When the judge saw the purse, he would stoop, pick it up, the bomb would explode—and there would be one less Supreme Court Justice to render decisions hostile to the Western Federation of Miners.

The bomb was planted. But on that particular morning Judge Gabbart took the long way around, using the sidewalk rather than the path. A while later a total stranger to Orchard—a man named Walley—came along, saw the purse, picked it up—and was blown into eternity.

At this point in the reading, Judge Goddard interrupts. He remembers the explosion. In fact, he remembers that Judge Gabbert later said to him, "I don't know what made me stay on the sidewalk that day. If I hadn't, I would have been killed instead of Walley."

"Wait," McParland tells Judge Goddard. "There's more."

Later in his confession, Harry Orchard states he later buried a bomb near Judge Goddard's gatepost, with its triggering device to be fired by a string leading up through a screw-eye fastened to the bottom of the gate. For some reason, the bomb did not go off. As far as Orchard knows, it is still buried by the judge's gate.

At this revelation, Judge Goddard becomes very agitated. Bulkley Wells, a Harvard engineering graduate, former Adjutant General of Colorado, and an explosive expert, is summoned, and the reading session is recessed to Judge Goddard's residence. After the family has been evacuated from the house, General Wells gingerly digs into the ground beside the gatepost, unearths the unexploded bomb, and carries it away to the arsenal for safe-keeping. It is indicative of the iron nerve of this man that he offers to bring the bomb intact to Boise as evidence in the trial, if need be. McParland tells him it will be permissible to remove its charge—before witnesses—and bring only the bomb case. Railroads and courtrooms, it seems, have some stuffy rules against live bombs.

Now McParland and Judge Goddard pay a call on the Governor of Colorado. Again the Harry Orchard confession is read. The governor asks McParland what is required of him. McParland points out that many of the crimes committed by Harry Orchard at the instigation of the Western Federation of Miners took place in Colorado. It would be possible to bring charges against Moyer, Haywood, and Pettibone and try them in Colorado. But a leading citizen of Idaho has been foully murdered. Idaho wants these men. Trials are expensive. Idaho, with the help of law and order men (meaning mine owners) is willing to bear the expense of the trial if it can get its hands on the criminals.

McParland has extradition requests from Governor Gooding, which swear that the wanted men were in Idaho at the time of the crime—in spirit, if not in person. He tells the Colorado governor if he will sign the necessary papers, he'll take care of the details.

Governor McDonald points out that, willing though he might be to grant extradition, the moment the papers are served on the three men, Western Federation of Miners attorneys will get writs of *habeas corpus*, which, with the inevitable appeals, will keep the men in Colorado indefinitely. Furthermore, the extradition papers must be filed in the attorney general's office; he is a strong pro-labor man, so the secret will be out in a matter of minutes.

McParland has the answer for that. Let the governor draw up and sign the necessary papers. Let special deputies be sworn in to make the arrests at 2 a.m. Sunday morning. Let a special train be ready and waiting on the outskirts of Denver. Let General Bulkley Wells be in charge of it. Let it leave Denver at 7 a.m. The courts will not be in session on Sunday. The train will be out of the state of Colorado before the

Western Federation of Miners realize what has happened. By dark Sunday night, the train will have crossed Wyoming and the birds will be safely flying across the state of Idaho. Then let the lawyers scream. As far as the labor-loving Attorney General is concerned, he'll get the papers on Monday.

Thus, it is arranged . . .

The three wanted men are being watched. At 9 p.m. Saturday night Moyer is seen at the railroad depot buying a ticket for South Dakota. McParland orders the three men arrested immediately, rather than waiting until 2 a.m. Sunday morning. The arrests are made. Haywood is found in bed in a "rooming house" with a woman not his wife. He has a loaded pistol on a nearby bureau, but is too surprised or otherwise occupied to use it.

The three men are hustled to the waiting special train. McParland wants it to move out at once, but the division superintendent of the Union Pacific says that is impossible. The train crews, clearances, and changes of engines have been set up for early Sunday. At this late hour, it is impossible to change the timetable. The train rolls north at 6 a.m.

In order to keep the hands of the Pinkertons clean, McParland has arranged for Colorado officers to make the arrests and for the special Idaho deputies to act as train guards, with General Bulkley Wells in charge. Wells declares that no law officer of less rank than a United States Marshal will be permitted to stop the train, and he is not at all sure that he would stop on even *that* officer's order. At any rate, there is only one U.S. Marshal that could possibly stop the train along the route it is taking; he lives in Cheyenne, Wyoming, which the train reaches at 10 a.m. Sunday morning.

The Cheyenne railroad yards have been cleared; the train, blinds on the passenger cars drawn, highballs through at thirty miles an hour. It is scheduled to cross Wyoming during daylight hours, stopping for coal and changes of crew only at isolated places. McParland reasons that a red lantern seen at night would make a stop mandatory, for a bridge might be out; in daylight, the engineer can see the track ahead.

Prisoners and guards are well supplied with fried chicken

and beer, the latter strictly controlled by General Wells. False trails and news stories have been planted back in Denver so the whereabouts of the three men is uncertain. As for McParland himself, he stays in Denver, feigning ignorance of the whole affair.

At a late hour Monday night, the three prisoners reach Boise City and are placed in the penitentiary for safe keeping. At about this same time, Steve Adams is located and arrested near Baker City, Oregon, and is taken to Boise . . .

Now the storm breaks in newspapers across the country, the labor press screaming "Kidnapped!" while the capitalistic press cries "Well done!" E. F. Richardson, Denver attorney for the Western Federation of Miners, takes a train to Boise and files a *habeas corpus* writ. Eugene Debs, a Socialist Party leader in Chicago, threatens to raise an army of 50,000 working men, lead it to Idaho, and liberate the prisoners by force of arms. Angry Idaho citizens answer, "Come ahead—we'll meet you at the border with hot lead."

Clarence Darrow, who has recently made a reputation for himself as a labor attorney, is called into the case to work with Richardson. The writ is denied in the lower courts, is appealed, and begins working its slow way upward toward the U.S. Supreme Court.

McParland returns to Boise and is disturbed to find one important detail of his complex plan has misfired. He has given specific instructions that Moyer is to be put in a cell separate from Haywood; he knows that Moyer is ill and has a seriously ill wife in California. He knows of a growing split between Moyer and the other two men. If given the opportunity, McPharland is sure that he can get Moyer to turn state's evidence, corroborate Orchard, and cinch the case against Haywood, Pettibone, and Simpkins, whose arrest he expects momentarily.

But the three men have been placed in the same cell. Moyer's backbone appears to have stiffened; the golden opportunity is lost. No matter. Steve Adams is available—and he is a weak man. McParland goes to work on him in the same manner he has worked on Orchard. In a matter of days, Steve Adams makes a full confession, not only corroborating most of what Orchard has said but adding a few murders in northern Idaho to which Adams was a party with the missing Simpkins . . .

By late February, 1906—two months after the murder of Frank Steunenberg—all the principals accused of the crime are confined in the Boise penitentiary. Both Harry Orchard and Steve Adams have signed detailed confessions. The charge against Moyer, Haywood, and Pettibone is conspiracy to commit murder, a capital offense, for which they must be prosecuted as principals. The defense has *habeas corpus* appeals pending; the prosecution has served notice that it intends to try Bill Haywood first, asking for the death penalty.

The ensuing year is a busy one as the prosecution tries to collect "independent evidence" that will corroborate details of the confessions and the defense tries to establish the fact that no evidence exists to connect the man on trial with the actual murderer. For example, in his confession Steve Adams describes how he was taught to make "Pettibone Dope," a liquid that bursts into flame when exposed to air.

Adams says several years earlier Haywood sent him to Pocatello, Idaho, with several jars of the liquid, which he was instructed to throw into a railroad car filled with strike-breakers due to pass through. Unable to accomplish his mission, he carried the evil-smelling jars into a vacant building just outside of town and buried them in the dirt floor. Now he is willing to take McParland to Pocatello and show him where the jars are buried.

Accompanied by Pinkerton detectives, prison guards, and a reporter from the *Idaho Statesman*, Steve Adams goes to Pocatello and supervises the search for the jars of Pettibone Dope. All the suspense elements of treasure hunt are here: changed landmarks, a burned-down building, abandonment of the search, the overhearing of a chance remark, a renewed search—and the eventual discovery of the jars which once contained the evil liquid.

In Harry Orchard's confession, states that two years previously Haywood sent him to San Francisco to murder Fred

Bradley, manager of the Bunker Hill & Sullivan mill at the time of the 1899 explosion. After an abortive attempt to poison Bradley by putting strychnine in his milk, Orchard planted a bomb at the door of the former mill-manager's apartment house, it exploded, threw Bradley into the street, and seriously injured him, but he recovered.

On checking the story, the Pinkertons learn there was indeed an explosion, but Fred Bradley thought it was caused by leaking gas rather than by a planted bomb. In fact, the owner of the apartment building has sued the San Francisco Gas Company and collected damages. Is Fred Bradley telling the truth? Is he trying to avoid trouble? Could there have been two explosions, first the bomb, then the gas from the ruptured lines? Most important, how can it be proved that Haywood and Pettibone were connected with the alleged attempt on Fred Bradley's life?

While these investigations by the prosecution staff are going on, and with the *habeas corpus* appeals still pending, Clarence Darrow arrives in Boise and confers with his associate-to-be, E. F. Richardson. Richardson is an extremely capable man, one of the finest criminal lawyers in the country, but a plodder. He has also been described as arrogant, opinionated, and temperamental. Clarence Darrow is unorthodox, amiable-appearing, but a keen student of human nature.

Richardson is a detail man, with a fine knowledge of law. Darrow is a gambler, going for the long-shot. He is said to have made the statement, "I'll do anything to win—even if it means bribing the jury," though the statement cannot be proved. Boise attorneys quickly dub him "Old Necessity"—for "necessity knows no law." Darrow and Richardson each believe themselves in charge of the case—a matter that will cause great friction in time to come.

Darrow sees at once that the most damaging part of the case to the defense is Steve Adams' confession, which corroborates Orchard's in many details. Adams has an uncle, invariably called "old man Lillard," living near Baker City, Oregon. Darrow pays him a call. Uncle and nephew are hill people who have migrated west from the Missouri Ozarks, ignorant, clannish, violent folk, with a long history of feuding and being "agin'" the government.

Details of just how Darrow works on Lillard are not clear, but it may be reasonably assumed that the attorney reminds the uncle of the hill code: "Better to die with sealed lips than live after informing on your clan."

Perhaps money changed hands—as was charged. Certainly it may be assumed that Darrow told the uncle that Steve Adams would have a more than even chance for life and freedom if he remained loyal to the Western Federation of Miners, while, if he testified against the organization in court, no power on earth could save him from assassination.

Whatever the method used, the net result of Darrow's talk with Lillard is that the old man goes to the penitentiary to see his nephew, has a heart-to-heart talk with him—and, shortly thereafter, Steve Adams repudiates his confession.

McParland is coldly furious. But there is a way to tighten the screws on Steve Adams, he points out to Borah and Hawley. In his confession, Adams has stated that with the help of Jack Simpkins he killed two timber-claim-jumpers in northern Idaho a few years earlier. When Adams is released from custody on a writ of *habeas corpus*, the sheriff of Shoshone County is waiting with a warrant for his arrest on a murder charge.

Central and northern Idaho are extremely mountainous; in those days, direct transportation by rail from Boise to Wallace was impossible. By rail, one could go east to Pocatello, north into Montana, then west to Wallace, Idaho; or one could go west into Oregon to Pendleton, north into Washington, then east to Wallace. Either way, the prisoner, Steve Adams, will have to be taken out of the state of Idaho—and the prosecution fears that the moment his physical person leaves the jurisdiction of the state of Idaho, *habeas corpus* writs will fall like manna from heaven.

McParland and Hawley make a "gentlemen's agreement" with Darrow and Richardson that no legal papers will be served while the prisoner is outside the state of Idaho. The defense attorneys board an Oregon-bound train; so do McParland and Hawley. But Steve Adams is not on it. During the dark of night, he has been quietly spirited out of the prison by the back entrance, and, accompanied by Warden Whitney, Sheriff Angus Sutherland of Wallace, and a couple of guards, is transported north across the mountains by a rugged stage, wagon, and horseback route that will require several days but will keep him within the boundaries of Idaho. McParland, it appears, does not think Richardson and Darrow are gentlemen.

The trial of Steve Adams in Wallace, Idaho, for the years-old murder of Fred Tyler, is a dress rehearsal for the main show soon to take place in Boise. Hawley and Borah act as special prosecutors; Richardson and Darrow conduct the defense.

In those days, filing timber claims in remote mountain areas, getting deeds to the land, then selling the land to big lumber barons, was a handy way to pick up a few dollars. Having such claims jumped was a hazard of the game. Getting shot for jumping—or for not jumping quick enough—was another.

A couple of men have disappeared and rumor has it that Steve Adams and Jack Simpkins have killed them. Some human bones and old clothes have been found, which are identified as the mortal remains of Fred Tyler. Reluctant witnesses give indefinite testimony; the jury deadlocks six and six; Steve Adams goes back into the Wallace jail to await a new trial.

Darrow is satisfied; he says he could hardly hope for an acquittal. McParland is satisfied; he says he could hardly hope for a conviction. But Steve Adams is still in the toils of the law, with the shadow of a noose hanging over him. Grimly, McParland goes back to work on him. The state will ask for a change of venue at the next trial, he points out to Adams. Next time, the trial will take place in a farming rather than a mining community; a jury of farmers will be sure to convict you. But if you will affirm your original confession . . .

Steve Adams remains sullenly silent.

Meanwhile, back in Boise, the legal maneuverings continue. The defense sets up an intricate trap, into which it hopes the prosecution will step. Earlier, the defense has filed *habeas corpus* writs for Haywood, Moyer, and Pettibone, which have been denied by the Superior Court. Appeals are taken to both the Idaho Supreme Court and the Federal District Court; both deny the appeals. The defense then files appeals with the United States Supreme Court from both lower court rulings. Noting that the appeals are identical, the Supreme Court combines them and sets an October 1906 date for the hearing, a date some months in the future. Now the defense sets up a clamor in the newspapers for an immediate trial of Haywood on the murder charge, claiming that the defense is ready but the prosecution is stalling.

This is potent propaganda, for by now the prisoners have been in confinement for many months. But Hawley and Borah refuse to step into the trap. They know that while a trial may be held pending an appeal from a state court decision, the U.S. Supreme Court has ruled that the result of a trial held pending an appeal from a Federal Court decision is null and void. Thus, the hands of the prosecution are tied until the U.S. Supreme Court makes its ruling on the appeals—unless the defense is willing to drop its appeal from the Federal District Court ruling and rest its case on the appeal from the State Court ruling. This Darrow refuses to do—and he makes dramatic capital of the fact that the prosecution has asked a man on trial for his life to surrender one of his constitutional rights.

In October 1906, the attorneys go to Washington, D.C. and argue the *habeas corpus* appeals before the United States Supreme Court. In late December, the Court hands down its ruling: appeals denied. The 8-1 ruling is based on two principles: (1) That an accused lawbreaker has no right of asylum in another state, and (2) That once his physical person is within the jurisdiction of the state accusing him of a crime, he must stand trial, regardless of the methods used to transport him into that state.

In a lone dissenting opinion, Justice McKenna calls the removal of the three accused men from Colorado to Idaho "kidnapping," but he bases his charge of illegality solely upon the fact that the Idaho extradition request has sworn that the accused were present in Idaho when the murder was committed—which they obviously were not. He overlooks the fact that Idaho law recognizes only principals, not accessories, and makes being present in spirit the same as being present in fact.

Now the rehearsals are over. A date is set for the opening performance—Bill Haywood's trial—before a blue-ribbon panel of critics, fifty top reporters for the nation's leading newspapers and magazines. . .

14

THE TRIAL OF BIG BILL HAYWOOD

A lthough the little town of Caldwell, Idaho, has enlarged and remodeled its courthouse in anticipation of playing host to what Eugene Debs calls "the most important trial in American history," the defense asks for a change of venue to another county. During the better part of a year, many residents and prospective jurors in southwestern Idaho have been receiving gratis copies of weekly papers such as the Socialist and the Appeal to Reason, both pro-labor publications whose chief purpose is to influence the readers in favor of the defendants.

Spies for both the prosecution and the defense swarm over the area, disguised as booksellers or insurance agents, talking to every possible juror—"ten percent books or insurance and ninety percent trial." They work in pairs so that they will be able to testify, if need be, that a certain prospective juror has discussed the trial and has formed an opinion. Alphabetical lists of names are made and behind each name are the letters: "N. G." or "O. K." Pinkerton men secretly work their way into the inner circle of the defense board of strategy and file reports by the number, such as: "Operative 21 Reports." It may be assumed that the defense also has its spies in the prosecution ranks.

In requesting a change of venue, the defense files over 600 affidavits as proof that potential jurors have formed and expressed an opinion. Judge Fremont Wood, who is to preside over the trial, states that while he is personally unconvinced that a fair, unprejudiced jury cannot be found in Canyon County, he will give the defense the change of venue which it has requested. The trial is slated to begin in Boise, Ada County, May 10, 1907.

Eight telegraph wires are leased to accommodate the newsmen; during the ten weeks that the trial lasts, 50,000 words a day are sent out to the press services of the world, which include the Associated Press, Reuters, and most of the metropolitan dailies. The selection of a jury requires almost three weeks, during which time 248 potential jurors are examined before a panel of twelve good men and true can be found. Most of the jurors are farmers and ranchers, union men being rejected by one side while bankers and businessmen are turned down by the other.

While the selection of the jury is still in progress, Governor Gooding permits a group of reporters to see and interview Harry Orchard at the prison, expressly stipulating that there are to be no questions regarding the forthcoming trial. Orchard makes such a favorable impression upon the reporters with his apparent truthfulness, sincerity, and religious conversion, he is given an extremely good press.

Richardson screams, "Foul!" Darrow chortles gleefully, "The sons-of-bitches will never get a jury in Ada County now!" Judge Fremont Wood is so fearful that this premature publicity may be grounds for a mistrial he orders an immediate investigation by Ada County Prosecutor Koelish to see whether contempt charges should be brought against the newswriters. Though the prosecuting attorney's reply is negative, Judge Wood verbally chastises the newsmen, and, by inference, Governor Gooding, McParland, Hawley, and Borah.

Errors in judgment are not confined solely to the prosecution legal staff. Soon after arriving in Boise, Clarence Darrow asks Judge Wood's former law partner, Edgar Wilson, to join the defense lawyer team, offering him a fat $15,000 fee. Wilson puts Judge Wood in an impossible position when he asks his

Idaho State Historical Society 534

Western Federation of Miners Union officials Charles Moyers, left, William Haywood, center, and George Pettibone were grabbed by authorities in Colorado and brought to Idaho under guard by special train.

old friend if his taking the job would in any way prejudice the judge's position. Judge Wood coldly tells him to let his conscience be his guide. After due consideration, Edgar Wilson accepts Darrow's offer—and then does nothing to earn the retainer except in the pre-trial examination of a couple of jurors. During the trial itself, Wilson does not once open his mouth in court, and much of the time is not even present.

Boise remains remarkably quiet. Rumors of mob violence, threats of assassination of Orchard by riflemen posted on the hills outside the prison, and bomb scares against the persons of Governor Gooding and Clarence Darrow—all prove to be as insubstantial as Eugene Debs' threatened army of 50,000 workers. In the labor press, Debs declares his intention to attend the trial as a spectator and one-man judge and jury but is dissuaded by Darrow and Richardson, who feel that his presence will do their client's cause more harm than good. Samuel Gompers, president of the conservative American Federation of Labor, is invited by Governor Gooding to attend the trial and witness the fairness of Idaho justice, but he stiffly declines. Gompers does not want his union identified with violence even by association.

A bearded, suspicious-looking man carrying a package is arrested as he tries to push his way into the crowded courtroom. When authorities question him and gingerly inspect the package, he is revealed to be a sheepherder just in from the hills carrying a dirty pair of overalls to his laundry woman.

Six attorneys sit at the defense table. All during the selection of the jury and the trial itself, Bill Haywood remains alert, constantly jotting down notes and conferring with Richardson and Darrow. Just behind him sits his family. His wife, a thin, pale woman who has been an invalid for the past eight years, is brought into court in a wheel chair a few minutes before each session begins, somberly dressed, accompanied by her sister, who acts as her nurse, her two daughters, thirteen and eight years of age, her mother, and Bill Haywood's own mother and father.

Behind the prosecution table, the murdered man, Frank Steunenberg, is not nearly as well represented. Following her collapse immediately after his death, Mrs. Steunenberg was gravely ill for a time, then, as she recovered, she was sent to Southern California where she has since lived with relatives most of the time. A deeply religious woman, she will appear in court for only one session during the entire trial—and then apparently much against her wishes. During the trial, she attends a Seventh Day Adventist Convocation in College Place, Washington, near Walla Walla, but the only comment she will make for the papers is that she cannot find it in her heart to condemn Harry Orchard. She hopes his religious conversion is genuine.

Julian Steunenberg, a young man of nineteen, appears in court and briefly testifies to having helped pick up the shattered body of his father and carry it into the house. Lieutenant William Steunenberg, a brother of the ex-governor, now stationed with the Army at Fort Lapwai, in northern Idaho, attends a session or two but says nothing for publication. The great actress, Ethel Barrymore, visiting Boise with a touring theatrical company, spends an afternoon in court while Harry Orchard is on the stand and is later quoted as saying that Orchard looks like a nice man, while Haywood's face frightens her half to death.

The trial transcript runs some 5,700 typed pages. Harry Orchard is on the witness stand for eight days. His story is that for years he has not worked as a miner; that he has killed enemies of the W.F.M. by gun, by bomb, and by the explosion of powder magazines—either on the specific instructions or with the specific approval of Bill Haywood and other members of the Executive Board. Whenever he needs money, he says, the Western Federation of Miners has supplied it.

To corroborate his story, the prosecution brings in witnesses from half a dozen states to prove that he has been where he said he was at such-and-such a time, that he has received money orders from George Pettibone and cash from Haywood, and that he is on friendly terms with what is called the "inner circle" of the organization. Orchard proves to be a good witness—calm, deliberate, factual; under intense cross-examination by the defense, he is never contradicted on any important detail.

The defense case depends chiefly upon proving that, while Bill Haywood knows Orchard as a union member and a frequent hanger-on around the Denver W.F.M. headquarters, they have never been intimate, no understanding exists between them, and no instructions to commit violence have ever been given him. Haywood also proves to be a solid, unshakable witness. On the stand, he makes a flat denial of everything tending to connect him with Harry Orchard in any violent way.

To combat the prosecution's contention that a conspiracy based on violence and murder exists in the W.F.M. inner circle, the defense attempts to set up a counter conspiracy on the part of the Mine Owners Association, which they claim is out to destroy union labor. Whenever a strike is called by a union, says the defense, the mine owners send in paid thugs and terrorists to blow up their own mine buildings and murder their own scabs, thus bringing in troops which persecute union men and run them out of the district.

The defense claims that Harry Orchard's entire confession is a tissue of lies; that many of the acts of violence he takes credit for were accidents; that he has been in the employ of the Mine Owners Association and their strong right arm, the Pinkertons; and that all the evidence brought in to corroborate his story has been planted by James McParland.

The defense does admit that Orchard murdered Frank Steunenberg, but it maintains that his motive for the killing is personal revenge. When Orchard first came to the Coeur d'Alenes in the 1890s, he bought an interest in a mine prospect called the Hercules, held on to it for a year or two, then sold it for a few hundred dollars. Since then, the Hercules has become an extremely rich mine and its current owners now are millionaires. The defense puts a dozen witnesses on the stand who swear that Harry Orchard has told them if it had not been for Frank Steunenberg's calling in the troops in 1899, which forced Orchard to leave the Coeur d'Alenes, Orchard would not have sold his interest in the Hercules and now would be a wealthy man. The dozen witnesses swear that Orchard vowed in their presence to kill Steunenberg.

This story has several serious flaws. In the first place, Orchard sold his interest in the Hercules in 1898, a full year before the Bunker Hill & Sullivan explosion forced Steunenberg to call in troops. In the second place, the dozen witnesses are people Orchard has met only casually—bartenders, rooming house ladies, strangers on trains, miners. Why would he express animosity toward ex-Governor Steunenberg to these people while not once has he expressed a similar sentiment to Bill Haywood, Charles Moyer, or George Pettibone, which they testify he has not? It is patently clear that the defense does not want to connect the W.F.M. board members with Orchard's alleged hatred of Steunenberg, though it is perfectly willing to show it through witnesses outside the charged conspiracy.

How much effect the fear of retaliation has on prospective witnesses is an imponderable element that may only be surmised. Conspiracy is a notoriously difficult charge to prove. If during a union meeting in Butte or Denver a man who thinks he has been abused by a Negro trooper by being rammed in the chest with a rifle, as Jack Simpkins claimed he was, should say, "That S.O.B. Steunenberg ought to be taken care of!", then Bill Haywood nods, Charles Moyer grunts something that sounds like assent, Harry Orchard overhears, and finally, after receiving $500 expense money from Haywood or Pettibone, plants a bomb on a gatepost six months later and accomplishes the expressed wish—is this a conspiracy? Perhaps. But even if it is, it must be proved that at a certain time and place certain words were said, money changed hands, and a definite understanding existed.

Witnesses living outside the state of Idaho cannot be forced to testify. During the trial, it is abundantly clear that prosecution witnesses are law and order people—that is, identified with the mine-owners' cause. It is equally clear that defense witnesses are people whose livelihood depends on the good will of the working man—the cause of union labor.

The prosecution insists that this is a murder trial, pure and simple. The defense claims that union labor is on trial, and that if Bill Haywood is convicted and executed he will die a martyr to a just and holy cause. The prosecution does not put the great detective, James McParland, on the stand; apparently it fears that cross-examination will bring out matters best left in the dark. The defense does not put George Pettibone or Steve Adams on the stand; apparently, it fears the same thing.

Opening and closing speeches by Hawley, Richardson, Darrow, and Borah are remarkable for their length, invective, and oratorical heights and depths—Darrow, for example, spoke for eleven hours. But it is doubtful their combined effect on the jurors approaches that of Judge Fremont Wood's firm and detailed instructions, which run some sixty-six typed pages.

After eliminating all defense evidence regarding a counter-conspiracy on the part of the Mine Owners Association as not sufficiently connected, and after ruling out material regarding the Steve Adams' alleged murder of the timber-claim-jumper for the same reason, Judge Wood carefully defines the charge of conspiracy and the limits as credible evidence of a murderer's confession unless solidly corroborated by "independent evidence."

The jury is out twenty-one hours. Its verdict: "Not Guilty."

When interviewed later by reporters, those jurors willing to discuss the trial and their reasons for voting as they did bring out the following points:

(1) They would not convict a yellow dog on the testimony of a wretch as debased as Harry Orchard.

(2) They could not make heads nor tails of Judge Wood's instructions, but they gathered he favored an acquittal. (3) They felt Bill Haywood was ". . . guilty as hell—but the State didn't prove it."

In mining camps across the West, the celebrations upon hearing the verdict are uproarious. In Chicago, New York, and other centers of Socialistic, Anarchistic, and Radical union sentiment, there is dancing in the streets. For the eighteen months before and during the trial, the labor presses of the United States, England, Europe, and Russia have been screaming: "Frameup! Rigged Trial! Capitalist Plot! No Justice for the Working Man!" and other such headlines. Parades of protest led by workers carrying the red flag of Socialism and Anarchy have been whipping Labor's appetite for a martyr into a frenzy.

In Butte, Montana, ten thousand Western Federation of Miners members march happily through the streets, shouting that justice has triumphed. Floating free on the breeze at the head of the procession are two proudly held, brand-new, red-white-and-blue American flags.

Like all great trials, the final verdict of this prolonged courtroom struggle can only be written by history after the passage of many years. Both capitalistic and labor presses agreed that Idaho, despite the loss of one of its leading citizens, had given Haywood a fair trial. Eugene Debs and other labor leaders tried to credit their red-hot editorials, protest marches, and the searing glare of publicity which they had turned upon the proceedings for Haywood's acquittal, claiming that the jury dared not convict. This is arrant nonsense, most historians agree. The jury stated its reasons for voting "not guilty." Lacking solid evidence to the contrary, those reasons should be accepted at face value.

Afterwards, Bill Haywood became a hero to the radical arm of the labor movement. He seemed to interpret the verdict to mean that violence was a legitimate tool in achieving labor's ends. For two decades thereafter, the battle between labor and capital was a sad and gory display of bombings, bullets, and the use of force.

Toward the end of World War I, Bill Haywood—now tied in hand and glove with the I.W.W.—was brought to trial on a sedition charge because of his advocacy of wartime strikes. While out on $25,000 bail, he skipped the country and fled to Russia. There, he lived out the rest of his days, a fugitive from his homeland. When he died in 1929, his body was cremated; honoring his last request, his ashes were interred in the Kremlin wall.

Clarence Darrow, who was paid $50,000 to defend the McNamara brothers for the dynamiting of the *Los Angeles Times* in 1910, which killed twenty employees, met the most serious reversal of his career when he was caught attempting to bribe a juror. To save himself and the lives of his clients, he was forced to advise them to admit their guilt—which they did.

Though he would go on defending the underdog the rest of his days—for a substantial fee—Darrow lost lustre off his halo following this humiliating defeat. Ample evidence exists that he came to hate Haywood and everything he represented.

Some months before the Haywood trial, President Theodore Roosevelt publicly called Haywood ". . . an undesirable citizen." The fact that the president had applied the same words to railroad magnate J. H. Harriman did not stem the storm of protest from labor leaders. Tens of thousands of badges were manufactured, sold, and worn by union men, proudly proclaiming: "I am an undesirable citizen."

William Borah's long career in the United States Senate as the "Lion of Idaho" is too well known to be detailed here. It is an ironic fact of history that Senator Borah—an iconoclast in so many ways—should have been one of the first prominent politicians to advocate the recognition of Russia.

James McParland's declining years were spent in routine detective work.

James Hawley later became Governor of Idaho. As a self-proclaimed "Sagebrush Lawyer," Hawley is one of those neglected figures of history whose abilities and achievements deserve better treatment than they have received.

Judge Fremont Wood, who had conducted the trial so fairly, was greatly criticized for his instructions to the jury, which led it to believe that a "Not Guilty" verdict was the only one acceptable to the court. A close study of those instructions reveals that, although he was leaning over backward to give the defendant the benefit of every doubt, the jury misinterpreted what Judge Wood was trying to tell them.

What he attempted to say was: "Orchard's confession must be corroborated before you can accept it as evidence." What the jury took him to mean was: "Disregard Orchard's confession and base your judgment on independent evidence alone." The distinction is a fine one, but it is there.

The conspiracy charges against Charles Moyer and George Pettibone eventually were dismissed. Jack Simpkins was never found. As a man who knew too much, as a man who had made several serious mistakes—such as sending Fred Miller to Caldwell to defend Orchard before his true identity was even known—Jack Simpkins was a highly dangerous man to have remain alive, so far as the W.F.M. was concerned. To this day, his fate is a mystery. But one cannot help but draw the conclusion that he left the country—or the world—unmourned.

Steve Adams was again tried on the old timber-claim-jumper murder charge, and again the jury disagreed. Taken to Colorado, Adams was tried on another murder charge, acquitted, and at long last turned loose.

It is interesting to note that not long after the final Adams' acquittal, the Oregon sheriff who first found and arrested him near Baker City was blasted into eternity by a bomb planted beside his gate. The sheriff's killer was never found.

Down in Colorado, another bomb destroyed the home of General Bulkley Wells, but Wells was not seriously injured. The bomb-planter was never found.

As to Harry Orchard himself, he finally was tried, found guilty, sentenced to death, then was given the commuted sentence of life imprisonment. He served it out in full measure, spending the rest of his eighty-four years behind the gray walls of the Idaho State Penitentiary in Boise. He died in 1956, a mellow, portly, gentle-eyed old man, who, as the years passed, became an expert on poultry, its diseases, and the art of egg-production.

During his early years in prison, one of his correspondent friends was a Walla Walla man named Daniel Gainey, who had lost both his feet in the Indepedence, Colorado, depot explosion, which Harry Orchard had set off. This man, too, had found solace in religion—and forgave Orchard his trespasses.

Perhaps it is academic at this late date to ask the question: "Did Harry Orchard tell the truth?" All reliable evidence indicates that he did. He murdered twenty men in cold blood, and maimed countless others; he did it at the instigation and with the approval of Bill Haywood and the Executive Board of the Western Federation of Miners.

Shortly before the trial began, a professor of psychology from Harvard—one Hugo Munsterberg—came to Boise, was granted an interview with Harry Orchard, and put the prisoner through a series of psychological tests. After the trial was over, Dr. Munsterberg published the results of his tests in *McClure's* magazine. In essence, they were word-associations tests, the results dependent not upon the answers but upon time-lapses between question and response. Dr. Munsterberg's conclusions were: first, that Harry Orchard was telling the truth, or at least what he believed to be the truth; and, second, that Harry Orchard had been emotionally dead for years.

Some years after the trial, Judge Fremont Wood—in summing it up—stated that he believed Harry Orchard had told the truth. It was possible for a witness to cook up a plausible story regarding a single event and stick to it through rigid cross-examination, Judge Wood said, but never in all his years on the bench had he known a witness to tell as long and involved a story as Harry Orchard had told and then make it stick together in all essential particulars as Orchard had done. . .

Under American law, there is no appeal from a verdict of "Not Guilty." But in the Bill Haywood case, the passage of time and the judgment of the unbiased researcher—if there be such a person—seems to recommend that the verdict be set aside and entered as it was expressed by one of the jurors: "Guilty as hell—but the State didn't prove it."

Certainly it was the right verdict at the time. If Bill Haywood had been hanged, the radical element of the labor movement would have been given the martyr it wanted and a wave of violence far more serious than what did happen during the next twenty years would have occurred.

In any case, the true victor seems to have been American justice.

* * *

BIBLIOGRAPHY

Blankenship, Russell, *And There Were Men*, Alfred A. Knopf, New York, 1942.

Borah, W. E., "Closing Argument, Haywood Trial," Boise, 1907.

Dimsdale, Thomas J., "The Vigilantes of Montana," published in the *Montana Post*, Virginia City, 1865, reprint by University of Oklahoma Press, Norman, 1953.

Gilbert, Frank T., *Historic Sketches of Walla Walla, Whitman, Columbia, and Garfield Counties*, Portland, 1882.

Grover, David H., *Debaters and Dynamiters*, Oregon State University Press, Corvallis, Ore., 1964.

Gulick, Bill, *Roadside History of Oregon*, Mountain Press, Missoula, Montana, 1991.

Snake River Country, Caxton, Caldwell, Idaho, 1971.

A Travelers History of Washington, Caxton, 1996.

Hailey, John, *History of Idaho*. Boise: Syms-York Co., 1910.

Haywood, William D., *Bill Haywood's Book*, New York, 1929.

Hawley, James H., *History of Idaho*. Chicago: S.J. Clarke, 1920.

Holbrook, Stewart H., *Rocky Mountain Revolution*, Henry Holt C., New York, 1956.

McParland, James "Reports, Haywood Investigation," Microfilm copy from Idaho State Historical Society.

McConnell, William J., *Early History of Idaho*. Caxton, 1913.

"The Idaho Inferno." Deposition, 1879, microfilm from Bancroft Library, University of California.

Orchard, Harry, Autobiography: *The Man God Made Again*, Southern Publishing Association, Nashville, Tenn., 1952.

Confession, Microfilm copy from Idaho State Historical Society, 1906.

Splawn, A.J., Kamiakin, *The Last Hero of the Yakimas*. Portland, Ore., Kilham Stationery & Printing Co., 1917.

Stone, Irving, *Clarence Darrow for the Defense*, Doubleday, New York, 1941.

Talkington, Henry L., *Heroes and Heroic Deeds of the Pacific Northwest*. Caxton, 1929.

PERIODICALS
Boise News, Idaho City
    Nov. 10, 1863.
    Feb. 13, 1864.

Feb. 20, 1864.
March 26, 1864.
June 25, 1864.
Idaho Statesman, Boise
Nov. 26, 1864.
Feb. 17, 1865.
Nov. 2, 1865.
Nov. 7, 1865.
Idaho World, Idaho City
Nov. 4, 1865.
Lewiston Teller, Lewiston
March 31, 1877
New York Tribune
Oct. 28, 1854.
Oregon Argus
May 19, 1855.
Nov. 24, 1860.
Walla Walla Statesman
Feb. 16, 1866
April 20, 1866.
April 27, 1866.

MICROFILM FROM IDAHO HISTORICAL SOCIETY
James McParland Reports, Harry Orchard Confession,
Transcript, Bill Haywood Trial, William Borah Closing
Argument, 1905-1907.

INDEX

A

Ada County Volunteers 2, 21-22
Adams, Steve 168, 173-174, 177, 187
Aden, Joseph 22
Alder Gulch 69, 88, 91, 113, 117, 119, 123, 128
Anderson, William T. 7, 10
Athena, Oregon 147, 152, 154, 157
Atlanta, Idaho 29

B

Bagg, Charles S. 120
Baker City, Oregon 173
Bannack, Montana 69, 72, 73, 79, 87-88, 91, 109-110, 113-116, 120, 123
Beachey, Hill 110, 112
Beidler, John X. 95
Bell, William H. 109, 112
Billings, Big Red 50
Billings, Booger Bart 49, 51
Blankenship, Russell 147, 149
Blue Mountains 16, 159
Bogus Basin 13
Boise Basin 42, 44-45
Boise City 1, 10, 13, 15, 17-19, 22, 24, 26, 33, 42, 107, 161, 173
Boise River 10
Borah, William E. 44, 163, 189
Bowen, Sheriff 40
Bradley, Fred 175
Brady, John 4
Brown, George 122
Brownlee Ferry 16
Bruneau Jim 3-4
Bunker Hill & Sullivan 162, 169, 175, 186
Bunton, Bill 122
Bunton, Sam 122
Burns, Dan 148
Burnt River, Oregon 148
Butte, Montana 72

C

Caldwell, Idaho 161-162, 166, 181
Canfield, J. T. 141-143
Carrhart, George 76
Carter, Alex 122
Cayuse Indians 147
Celilo Falls 56
Chang Yen Hoon 140
Chea-Cheong 138
Chea-Chow 138
Chea-Lin-Chung 138
Chea-Ling 138
Chea-Po 138
Chea-Shun 138
Chea-Sun 138
Chea-Yow 135-136, 138, 146

Cheyenne, Wyoming 172
Chico, California 1
Chief Bigfoot 1, 4-8, 11-12
Chief Joseph 139
Clark, John C. 23
Clark, W. M. 142
Cleveland, Jack 73, 75, 83
Cold Spring Ranch 116
Colonel Wright 56-58, 60
Columbia River 56, 58
Cooper, Johnny 122
Couer d'Alene, Idaho 162
Cover, Tom 88
Crawford, Hank 74-75, 83, 85-86
Crook, General George S. 10
Crutcher, Sheriff 40, 42
Cynthia 101-103, 105, 108

D

The Dalles Mountaineer 158
Daniels, William 111
Darrow, Clarence 173, 175, 182-183, 189
Dart, George 87
Davenport, I. W. 74
Davis, Alexander 120
Day, John 136
Debs, Eugene 173
Deer Lodge 84
Dempsey's Ranch 116, 118
Deschutes Landing 56
Dimsdale, Thomas 68-69, 72, 93, 97
Dixon, Jake 26
Donahue, Hugh 45-47
Duffy, C. M. 48
Dutch Jo 55, 62, 64

E

East Oregonian 151, 158
Elk City 48
Evans, Bruce 142-143

F

Fairweather, Bill 88
Fiddler John 6
Flint, Idaho 3
Florence, Idaho 48, 103, 105, 107
Forbes, Charley 89, 91-92
Fort Boise 2, 22, 34, 41-42
Fort Lapwai 184
Fort Walla Walla 58-59, 101

G

Gabbart, Justice 170
Gallagher, Jack 89-90, 92, 95, 129-132
Gibbons, Johnny 119
Gilkey, John 43
Goddard, Justice 170
Gompers, Samuel 183
Gooding, Frank R. 162-163, 165-166, 171, 183

Goodrich's Saloon   73, 77, 79
Goose Creek Mountains   9
Graves, Whiskey Bill 122

H

Hailey, John   5, 98, 149
Hart, Deputy O. J.   148
Hauser, Sam   86
Hauser, Samuel T.   113
Hawley, James   163
Haywood, William (Big Bill)   164, 167-169,
      179, 184-186, 189,
      191-192
Hells Canyon   137, 139
Helm, Boone   122, 129-130, 132, 134
Henry Plummer Gang   100, 103, 109,
      113
Highland, Montana   129
Hilderman, George   116, 127-128
History of Idaho   5
Hogan, Thomas   163, 167
Horseshoe Bend, Idaho   18
Horsley, Albert (Harry Orchard) 167
Howard, David   111
Hughes, Barney   88
Hughes, Carl   141-143
Hung Ah Yee   140
Hunter, Bill   122, 129
Hurdy-Gurdy Girls   57
Hyer, Henry   68, 70

I

Ice Harbor 61
Idaho City, Idaho   29, 32, 34, 37, 40, 42,
      44-45
Idaho Statesman   7, 19, 45, 175
Idaho World   45
Imnaha River   139
Ives, George   74, 76, 116-118, 122,
      127-128

J

Johnson, Jack   36
Jordan Valley   2
Joseph, Oregon   146
Junction, Montana   129

K

Kelly, John   6
Kelly, Judge Milton   42
Kimbrough, Sheriff Luke   49, 51
Kingsley, Elder   43
Kong-Mun-Cow   138
Kong-Ngan   138

L

Lane, Clubfoot George   122, 129-130,
      132
Langford, Nathaniel   78, 80, 97-98, 109
LaRue, Homer   141-142
LaRue, Mat   143
Lee Loi   141
Lewis, Joe 9
Lewiston, Idaho   56, 61, 72, 110, 112, 135,
      141

Log Cabin Bar   140
Lolo Trail 112
Long, Charlie   156-157
Los Angeles Times   189
Lower Granite Dam   135
Lowry, D. C.   111
Lyman, W. D.   47
Lyon, Governor Caleb 13, 20, 22
Lyons, Haze   89, 91, 94-95, 122, 129,
      132

M

MacNeal, Hugh   72
Maddock, Sheriff Frank   148
Magruder, Lloyd   109
Marcus, Charley   17
Marshall, Colonel L. H.   10
Marshall, Major   20
Marshland, Steve   122
Masons   109-110, 112
Mayfield, Bill   101, 107
Maynard, H.   141-142
Maynard, Hiram   143
McBride, Judge John 42
McConnell, William J. (Billy)   14-16, 18, 21,
      44-45, 98
McKenna, Frank   165
McMillan, Robert   141-142, 144
McParland, James   165, 168, 172, 176, 187
Mexican Frank   122
Miller, Fred   164, 169
Mitchell, William   77
Montana Post   69
Montana Territory   69
Moore's Creek   37
Moore, Bill   77, 80
Moore, Gad   122
Moyer, Charles   168-169, 186, 190
Munsterberg, Hugo   191

N

Nam-puh (Bigfoot)   4
Nevada City, Montana   71, 117, 129
Nez Perce Crossing   139-140
Nez Perce Reservation   56

O

Orchard, Harry   167-170, 185-186, 190
Orofino   61, 72
Otter (Utter) Massacre   9
Owyhee   14, 20, 136
Owyhee Mountains   1
Owyhee Volunteers   3

P

Page, Billy   111-112
Parker, Six-Toed Pete 49, 51
Parks, Judge Samuel C.   112
Parrish, Frank   122, 129, 132, 134
Patterson, Ferd   30, 36, 38, 40, 42, 45, 107
Patton, W. H.   119
Payette River   18, 44
Payette Valley   14
Payette Valley Vigilantes   14, 18
Payne, D. S.   113

Pemberton, W. Y.   120
Pendleton, Oregon   149, 152, 155, 158
Peters, Gil 15
Pettibone, George   167-169, 185-186, 190
Pike, Tom 111-112
Pine Grove   129
Pinkerton Agency   163
Pinkham, Sumner   32-33, 35, 38-40, 43, 45
Pioneerville, Idaho   29
Placerville, Idaho   14-15, 29, 107
Plummer Gang   83, 86-87, 97-98, 111, 127-128
Plummer, Henry   43, 68, 70-71, 73, 75, 78-79, 83-84, 86-88, 96, 112, 114, 118-119, 121, 124
Porter, Deputy   100
Portland, Oregon   56, 111
Prineville, Oregon   156

R

Rattlesnake Ranch   78
Ray, Ned 88, 122
Raymond, Rube   22-23
Reeves, Charley   74, 77, 80
Reynolds Creek   2, 20, 22
Richard Bogle   45, 47, 49-50, 52, 54
Richardson, E. F.   173
Robbins, Orlando (Rube)   40-41, 43-44
Rocky Bar   14, 26, 29
Romain, Ames   111

S

Salt Lake City, Utah 72
Sam Yup Company   138, 140
Sanders, Wilbur F.   120
Saratoga Hotel   161, 163
Seven Devils Mountains   139
Shear, George   122
Silver City, Idaho   1, 164
Simpkins, Jack   167-168
Skinner, Yrus   122
Slim Jim   49-54
Snake River   1, 9, 14, 58, 139
Standifer, Jeff   4
Sterling, Will   159-160
Steunenberg, Frank   161-162, 174, 186
Steunenberg, Julian   184
Steunenberg, William 184
Stinson, Buck   89, 91, 95, 122
Stohlhofen, Hans   57-58, 60-61
Stuart, Granville   98
Summit, Montana   129
Sun River Farm   73
Sutton, T. J.   4

T

Talbert, Cherokee Bob   72, 100-102, 104-106
Terwilliger, Billy   122
The Dalles, Oregon   56
Theodore Roosevelt   189
Thiel Agency   163
Thurmond, J. M.   120

Tong Society   138
Tyler, Fred   177

U

Umatilla Indian Reservation   147
Updyke Gang   17
Updyke, Dave   15-16, 19, 21, 23, 26

V

Vaughan, Hank   147-148, 150, 154, 157, 159-160
Vaughn, Frank   141, 143
Vegetable Peddler   14
Vigilante Days and Ways   79, 97
Virginia City, Montana   69, 72, 79, 89, 93, 95, 114-116, 120, 127, 129, 131

W

Wagner, Dutch John 122
Wagner, John P.   151
Walla Walla Union   141
Walla Walla, Washington   14, 45, 47, 52, 59, 61, 63, 65, 72, 99-100, 110, 159, 184
Wallace, Idaho   177
Wallowa Mountains 139
Wallula Landing   58-59, 61, 111
Ward Party Massacre 9
Warm Springs   33, 37
Weiler, Governor John P.   70
Wells, Bulkley   171-172, 190
Wells, Dr. Merle   136
Western Federation of Miners   162, 164, 168-170, 172, 191
Wheeler, John   8, 10
White, Captain Leonard   58
Whitley, Doc   150, 153
Whitman Massacre   9
Wilkinson, Archer   9
Wilkinson, Starr (Bigfoot)   9
Williams, Jakey   106
Willoughby, Bill   104-105, 107
Wisconsin Creek   118
Wolfe, Josephine   55-56, 59, 61, 63
Wood, Judge Fremont 182, 187, 190-191

Y

Yankee Flat   109
Yellowstone National Park   79

Z

Zachary, Bob   122

THE AUTHOR

Bill Gulick

Bill Gulick is considered by many to be the dean of Northwest history writers. During a career spanning more than half a century, Bill has written more than thirty books, five movie scripts and more than 200 articles and stories for newspapers, national magazines and television.

Outlaws of the Pacific Northwest is the fifth Gulick nonfiction book published by *Caxton Press*. The others, all still in print, include *Snake River Country, Chief Joseph Country* and *A Traveler's History of Washington* and *Manhunt: The Pursuit of Harry Tracy*.

Gulick's novel, *Roll On, Columbia,* an historical trilogy, was recently released by Colorado University Press.

A long-time Washington state resident, Gulick has won numerous regional and national awards. He was one of the founders of the Western Writers of America.

For a free Caxton catalog write to:

CAXTON PRESS
312 Main Street
Caldwell, ID 83605-3299

or

Visit our Internet Website:

www.caxtonprinters.com

Caxton Press is a division of The CAXTON PRINTERS, Ltd.

WC